# THE 5TH PHENOMENON

Awareness Field Theory
and the
Structured Orders of Consciousness

## Robert A. Revel

Cool Tribe World® Publishing
Santa Rosa, CA

Copyright © 2018 by Robert A. Revel

All rights reserved. No part of this book may be reproduced or transmitted in any form or by any means, electronic or mechanical, including photocopying, recording, or by any information storage or retrieval system, without permission in writing from the publisher, except by reviewers, who may quote brief passages in a review.

Published by

Cool Tribe World® Publishing
131 A Stony Circle, #500
Santa Rosa, CA 95401

Cover artwork
Lenni Revel

Cover and text design
Caren Parnes, Enterprising Graphics

Editing
Caren Parnes, Enterprising Graphics
Abra Bragg

ISBN 978-1-7322717-0-8

Library of Congress Control Number: 2018943571

Printed in the United States of America

This Book is Dedicated to Lenni.

*"Alas, I am nothing without her,
save the something that came to love her."*

*Algebraic signature for Full Spectrum Consciousness as presented in Awareness Field Theory*

*According to my calculations, I know nothing—that is all.*
–Awareness Field Theory maxim

# THE 5ᵀᴴ PHENOMENON

*Awareness Field Theory*
*and the Structured Orders of Consciousness*

| | | |
|---|---|---|
| *Prologue* | | *vii* |
| *Introduction* | | *xi* |
| 1. | Clarity | 1 |
| 2. | An Extraordinary Life | 9 |
| 3. | Introduction to Awareness Field Theory (AFT) | 15 |
| 4. | Noumenal Awareness | 21 |
| 5. | Quantum Field Presence | 29 |
| 6. | Temporally Positioned Consciousness | 37 |
| 7. | Conversion Portals | 47 |
| 8. | Systems | 57 |
| 9. | Human Sentience | 69 |
| 10. | Being | 83 |
| 11. | God | 91 |
| 12. | Existential Schisms & Mental Health | 101 |
| 13. | Philosophy, Consciousness, Spirituality & Self Help | 113 |
| 14. | Sexuality | 139 |
| 15. | Love | 147 |
| 16. | The Lens | 155 |
| 17. | The Way Out | 171 |
| 18. | Listening | 179 |
| 19. | Transmission | 191 |
| 20. | Surrender | 197 |
| 21. | We the People | 203 |
| Afterword: "The Reply" | | 213 |
| Glossary of AFT Terms | | 237 |
| About the Author | | 251 |

# Prologue

I remember the day I turned sixteen. I looked up at the heavens and proclaimed that it was the perfect age, and that I might not mind if I were to stay that age forever. I really loved the idea of it somehow. What I didn't know is that my 16th year would bring something that would change my life forever. That year I would be introduced to a wheelchair-bound woman in her 80s. Her name was Alice H. Simms, and I met her through my job delivering flowers for a local florist company. She was an extraordinary woman with a fire in her eyes seldom seen in human beings. Like all auspicious relationships, the moment we first met I recall clearly in my mind to this day.

I walked up the small rise of steps to the metal landing of the trailer home's rickety porch. The front door was open and through the screen I could see an elderly woman sitting at a small card table. She looked over at me standing there with flowers, and with a furrowed brow, waved me in.

"I have some flowers here for Alice Simms. Is that you?" I offered. She looked at the flowers momentarily. "Put them over there on the counter," she replied. Then, rather nonchalantly, she looked back down at the papers in front of her and began to speak without lifting her gaze from the documents.

"Must be my grandson. He loves sending those things... makes him feel better for not coming around to see the old girl." She looked up at me and smirked. Her gaze was uncommonly direct. In time I would come to know intimately the piercing quality of her eyes, and how they could look right through you without shifting away from her own grounded essence.

She looked back down at her papers as she grabbed a magnifying glass to peruse the writing in one specific area of the document. I began taking in the surroundings of her little mobile home, finally settling in again on the rather dog-eared documents she was scanning in front of her. The papers were old and yellowed with manual typewriter print on them. As I focused in on the brittle parchment I saw the title on the page she was reading said "The Power of Truth."

What? I thought. The power of truth? What is that about? And why is this elderly woman reading it? It was at that very moment that she looked up and caught my eyes scanning the manuscript in front of her. "Does that interest you?"

"I'm sorry. I didn't mean to...." I began contritely, as she raised her hand to stop me.

She looked me up and down. "What's your name, young man?"

Thus began a ten-year relationship in which I would visit Alice, usually several times a week, to sit and talk about the true nature

## Prologue

of human consciousness. I would cherish our visits until the day she died.

Alice would often ask rhetorically: "What is this subtle pretext of purely mortal error?" She seemed always to say this with her brow furrowed and her eyes burning with intensity. At 16 years of age I didn't really get the gravity of the inquiry. Now, 35 years later, I know the power of that question, and how it probes into the core of our human dilemma. I at last understand why she always delivered that query with such ferocity and presence. Perhaps she knew that I was one day destined to bring forward to the world an answer to that question—a riposte from the kid that might have even made the old girl smile. If this book is a fire, I will tell you without hesitation, that woman was the spark. ✪

# INTRODUCTION

*"…compared to eternity…all things are diminutive, subject to change and decay… yet all things proceed from…the One Intelligent Cause."*
—Marcus Aurelius, Emperor of Rome, 121-180 CE

Is violence a natural occurrence, or is it the mark of a struggling species? Today, nearly all of the current global challenges we face have been brought about by human conduct. Have we as complex creatures lost touch with something essential to our evolution and gone severely astray? In some respects it could be argued that we have even begun to display a peculiar form of de-evolution. One may fairly inquire as to whether the human race might actually be falling short of its intended design potential. In holding to that premise, a significant question arises: What are we missing? Whatever it is we are overlooking, we may do well to consider what crucial insights it will afford the human condition when found. How would such a critical discovery inform and nourish us, and how might it change our future outlook for the better? This book is committed to unveiling, and detailing that elusive piece.

We are creatures of thought. The ability to conceptualize is a powerful tool, yet we have made it our sole and primary reality—

giving rise to the most basic and fundamental error of our existence. We are meant to perceive deeper than the mind's mere data processing and projection capacities. We have somehow missed that our moment-to-moment consciousness is predestined to be enriched by much more than the brain's conceptual framework. We have built a thick wall where there used to be a window to light, space, and the ephemeral wisdom of the universe. That wall is born of thought.

This book is about a movement, a journey into our essential nature to apprehend the multiple fields of awareness that exist prior to thought. This project will reference some of the finest minds that humanity has ever produced, to examine what has so far been revealed on the subject of human sentience. Then it will plunge out beyond, across the threshold of the mind's limitations, and into the open Presence that abides outside of and within thought. In this place we discover the portal inside our consciousness that allows fluid access to a flow of Primordial Intelligence—the "One Intelligent Cause," Aurelius speaks of in this chapter's opening quote. By revealing the uncultivated transparency that accesses the depths of our consciousness, *The 5<sup>th</sup> Phenomenon* exposes the missing link that will unleash the full potential expression of humanity for the next age

This book may be a new reading experience for you. At times it is an academic treatment, and at other times a reflective memoir. There are poetic moments that have the feel of sutra-like ruminations. Some chapters reference relevant segments of history, and the afterword even offers a fictional foil to Russian novelist Fyoder Dostoyevsky's (1821-1881 CE) finest work. Ultimately, this book

## Introduction

was deliberately designed to move outside of convention in both structure and content. I invite you to be open, and let the book, like a wild river, float you to that place inside yourself wherein the real answers lie.

Though erudite at times, this book does not contain footnotes or cite scholarly authority to bolster and affirm its points and reflections. You are the authority as the reader, as I am quite simply the author who is presenting it. In that place we are both sovereign, and we do not require sanction from the scrutiny of anyone to discern and determine what is ultimately true for ourselves—specifically with regard to the ineffable content we will explore. In the end we must find our own way back to the Source that created us, if we are to acquire genuine *clarity*. I am a great fan of clarity. The search for clarity is more sublime, and certainly less provocative than the search for truth, because seeking clarity is not about establishing universal absolutes. A desire to see clearly and without distortion is an endeavor that is less prone to polarization from others. Even the clarity around moments of uncertainty lead gently to a benevolent curiosity that provides no fuel for conflict. So with an intention to become profoundly clear about this existence, I invite you on a journey into *The 5th Phenomenon*.

# CHAPTER 1
## Clarity

I'm sitting on the stoop of my grandmother's house in the Hunter's Point district of San Francisco circa 1974. The sun is out, and warm all over my body. At this moment, I don't feel hungry, or tired, or sore, or worried, or bored. There is nothing missing. In this moment I feel that specific kind of lightness of being that can only come with being 9 years old on a sunny summer day. I'm not thinking about God, but in this unencumbered moment I feel clearly the Presence of the Creator. It is as real as the warmth and light of the sun on my body. What I sense is a living thing, not an idea or a concept-deity like the one they are talking about in church. That god was always something foreign to my nature, thrust into my world by people that felt strange and possessed of something heavy and unnatural. But there is nothing outside of *this* Presence I feel here and now, and I can perceive it moving everywhere all at once. I close my eyes and swim in the body of it.

This feeling, and a million other still moments just like this in my childhood are the ongoing hallmark of my inner experience as a kid. Though interior peace often runs in stark contrast to the external environments of my youth, the resonance of that sublime connection never wanes—it never forsakes me. As a child, I tend not to speak about it around others. In one sense, it seems unnecessary to relate something that is to me quite obvious, but I also quickly decipher that this feeling does not appear to be a common topic with people, so in keeping it to myself I learned to avoid the inevitably unfulfilling gesture of trying to relate it.

Forty years later, that secret is no longer the private and solely internal matter it was when I was a child. Now it is the foundation for how I move in the world, so there is no way to hide it. That peaceful place I once had no name for, indeed had no *need* to name in my youth, now oddly requires concepts and labels to extrapolate and share with others as an adult. So to keep it simple, I call it *clarity*. Clarity is not a philosophy, nor is it a religion. Neither is it some edification of mystical spirituality. Clarity came to be a consistent personal theme in my life because, ultimately, clarity means *to see without distortion*. To know clarity is to directly experience this life without the current plague of psychic bewilderment that affects us as a species. The fog of unconscious living descends upon us all along the journey as an inevitable part of the process of living out our lives. For me, one burning question routinely served to dissolve those persistently accumulating mists of confusion by bringing my focus back to clarity: *What is happening in this existence?*

As the years unfolded, and the inquiry grew more and more intense, I searched everywhere for an intellectually fulfilling answer.

# Clarity

I found that no one, living or dead, had delivered a comprehensive revelation that fully satisfied *me*. The dilemma this unfulfilled query posed in my life ultimately led me to abandon searching externally for an answer that never would appear "out there." It caused me to inquire within. The understanding that I so feverishly sought would have to come from the questioner himself, or at least my capacity to access the Source Intelligence that is capable of answering such a profound inquiry. In reflection, I can now see that as important as answers are, the sincere act of asking the right *question* is what produced the correct heading toward real clarity in my life. For it is the heading, and not the arrival, that constitutes the substance of our journey.

In great measure, it is the force and scope of the aforementioned question that has driven this book to fruition. Personally, this book does answer the question, *what is happening here?* At the same time, I recognize that no singular examination could be an absolute telling of the total story of being human; nor is it a complete treatise on our existence as a species. What this book does accomplish is the establishment of a clear invitation to begin coherent dialogue around an art form that I sense we all need to engage and explore. That artful expression beckons us into a fully dimensional experience of consciousness; one that summons an individual's perception to move beyond just a clever collection of ideas designed to create personal identity or pursue intellectual intrigue.

Intrigue is a type of curiosity that serves to entertain the personality by formulating provocative notions of what it sees, and about what is right and what is wrong. That kind of curiosity is useless precisely because there are no *complete* truths in the conceptual realm. Over and above the many ideas explored in this book, it is the passionate search for clarity itself that is of paramount significance—and clarity is a quality of perception, not a statement of position or fact. Rational doctrines have in fact become a hollow panacea for human confusion and fear that often turn out to be more distracting than helpful. *The 5th Phenomenon* is my attempt to cut to the bone; to find something more complete and useful that begins to respond to an inquiry that we can no longer afford to sidestep. In plunging the necessary depths I intend to reveal critical insights relating to the most intimate and essential aspect of our existence—consciousness itself.

If you have an almost radical longing for living authentically out of real clarity, I trust that this book will have something important for your considerations. I also trust that we would personally find rapport with or without this book. Our kindred resonation would arise from the certain order of honesty with which we seek and explore. I posit that thoughts expressed, and actions taken, without such a cradle of sincerity can even prove dangerous. People will build cults around even the most inspired ideas when desultory agendas are part of the equation. There has been more human blood spilt on this planet over ossified ideologies in opposition than for any other reason. Wars are rarely fought over a genuine need for food or shelter; they are routinely fought over contradictory belief structures—those typically being political, cultural or religious.

The highest form of intellectual expression exhibits consciousness that is free from doctrinal ideas that espouse absolute positions. I advocate communion with the pure Creator Intelligence that transcends our mass psychosis; that disease which is born from the error of fragmented thought systems. I know from direct experience that it is a radical proposition to let go of the sacred cows of conceptual paradigms and stand naked to life with just a sincere inquiry that longs only for the clarity of Presence to reconcile and inform it. Genuine longing, though emotionally wrenching at times, is void of inner conflict. Certainly, the dramas in my life's story have come not from Presence ever abandoning me, but from me forsaking it.

Getting older, and heavier with the conceptual culture of mankind weighing me down as the years went by, I had learned about life in broken pieces that were spoon-fed to me by a disconnected society. Eventually I got distracted from the natural magic that only comes with sensing the whole. For a while, I too partially forgot about the sublime rapture of humble surrender to the moment that came to me so organically as a child. Like so many of us, over the years I took up with the ill company of a time-locked world, where fantasy, fear, control and rage made up some portion of every second that went by. Unwittingly, and by degree, I became indoctrinated into this common condition of unnecessary confusion. I, like most of my fellow human beings, became saturated with the rampant distortions that the bulk of humanity wallows in every day.

I think we all feel the shock of being in this world. In so many ways this existence can feel appalling to our sensibilities. Even for the so-called privileged, there is no core insulation from the powerful winds that blow through our conceptual shutters and find their swirling way into our trembling psyches. Life is not always a rainbow romp through sun-drenched fields of wildflowers and butterflies. In my youth, I observed that there seemed to be no one who was *truly* at peace with it all. Who, I wondered, might I utilize as a model for how to cope with all that I had already seen and felt, in even my young life? Where was the contented soul who could see and deeply feel this world without contraction? And not just some somberly contemplative individual cloistered in a remote hermitage, but someone passionately engaged—enjoying a reverie of communion with others, while moving productively in the world. Where too, was the village sage? And not just some professorial lecturer of stale facts, but the luminously imbued soul, burning with a shamanistic wisdom.

Today I still ask these questions. I look out into the cultural landscape, hoping for signs of such vital spirits living among us; I listen for word of them, even third or fourth hand. My current longing for these connections is different than when I was younger. Now it comes from a desire to commune with kindred souls, and not merely to help rescue me from the many confusions I once knew. But to find such rare individuals is no easy task. As it turns out, really clear and genuine people don't tend to promote themselves. Marketing, after all, is a pursuit reserved for those who have something to sell. But the radiant sojourners *are* out there, and growing in number with each new generation. You yourself may make up the *esprit de corps* of that shining world tribe. This book will go on to suggest that in many different ways, we are all at the dawn of unfolding a new order of conscious community.

Feel into it. We can offer the next generations something different than what we knew growing up. We can present to those children a world full of authentic spirits who are determined to arrive at, and sustain, serene clarity. We can model for them a different potential to exist in a vital contentment without the decades of mind-bending distortion and heart-wrenching desperation we have all experienced. We can demonstrate for them how we may achieve a deep reconciling with the remarkable spectacle of nature, while not getting stuck in the tangle of conceptual paradigms that haunted our ancestors. But it will require a new direction, a change in course that this book is dedicated to help calculate. It is then that we will find ourselves on a direct heading toward an encounter with clarity as individuals and as a world community—an event that will unfold the next chapter of human evolution. Such a movement would deconstruct the safe and familiar faux realities of current mass consciousness and release us into the freedom that is inherent in our design as creatures of unique radiance.

If you long for a world where we all move in genuine clarity—and want that even more than attaining an idea of some method of enlightenment, then I invite you to read on. I recognize fully that it isn't easy to be truly authentic and clear—but then what is? There is an old saying, "The right way takes just as much energy as the wrong way." Perhaps. But for myself, it is much more *interesting* to be clear than to be right—no matter how much energy it takes. When the path is sincere, Life gives us what is necessary for the journey—be it courage or water. Fear not, Life is present with you. ✪

# Chapter 2
# An Extraordinary Life

How often do we compare our own experience in life with the performance of others? We see a varied landscape of human achievement, and may be in awe of the accomplishments of certain individuals that garner our esteem. Whether historic or contemporary figures, all of us are drawn to look for examples of souls who seem to hold the key to living fuller lives while suffering less.

We are attracted by certain qualities because we sense that they give rise to results we admire and long for ourselves. It may be a peaceful essence that pervades their personality. It may be an imperturbable benevolence, ever-present in their disposition. It may be an unbridled passion that infuses all their actions; a gift that seems to bring abundance everywhere they direct it. It may be a sterling integrity that moves absolutely outside corruption and compromise. Or it may be an abiding compassion whose goodwill seems to have a healing and restorative effect on all within its influence. Wherever we identify these individuals and the rare and numinous qualities they reflect, we inevitably find them inspiring to our weary souls.

We may appreciate such individuals personally, but that reverence alone will not actualize the qualities we long for in ourselves. We must look beyond the personalities of these exceptional people and direct our attention deep into the craft of living that those amazing figures have somehow awakened to. For we may fairly ask, do they really *know* more than we do, or have they simply cultivated access within themselves to something larger than who they are as mere individuals? Are they somehow being infused and inspired by a source transcendent of themselves? If this is indeed the case, and I suggest that it is, then the key to the art of living is not to emulate those that are successful, or even to simply accumulate their knowledge or skillsets, but instead to discover the art of tapping into the same nourishing current that elevates their performance in the world to one we recognize and acknowledge as extraordinary. Such an endeavor is no casual task—it becomes a passionately lifelong affair that presents to us a horizon that changes moment to moment.

As incarnate beings, we live on a timeline between the organic bookends of birth and death. We endure the vicissitudes of chemistry, physics and time that are inherent in the phenomenal universe we are born into. We all feel the tension of pushing out into life with our sentient forms as we struggle to hone the craft of living. Simply existing in the physical world—to be in a body on this planet—is one hell of a proposition. This book explores the notion that an effective existence requires an understanding of the fields of awareness that animate life; a wisdom that allows us to artfully navigate the full dimension of consciousness itself. In doing so we naturally elevate our performance.

As we begin to unfold an understanding of the operational systems of sentience that animate life, something large and unavoidable is revealed: The multi-dimensional structure of awareness fields I refer to as *The 5th Phenomenon*. The articulation of these awareness systems as a fundamental and universal phenomenon is the primary subject of this treatise. I present these specific operational awareness features in the universe through a postulate I call Awareness Field Theory (AFT). In addition to a detailed exploration into the heart of human sentience, the exposition also leads us to the very structural fabric and framework of the universe we occupy. Traveling through a range of scientific and philosophical terrain, we will routinely meet with the critical theme of conscious potential available to us as human beings, through a call to Presence the majority of our species has yet to realize.

Along the way we will explore what takes an ordinary life and makes it extraordinary, and elucidate how such a quality of existence is universally available to all of us. Within these pages you will find a conceptual outline of the key to living out your full potential. It is the birthright of all human beings to live deeply at peace with themselves. Ultimately, though, it is the choices we make around the opportunities and insights we are given that determine the quality of our existence. One thing is certain however—we are more than brutes. We are more than fearful and confused creatures huddled in the dark. We are more than a congregation of mediocre and half-lived lives of little meaning and consequence. We are more even than the accomplishments of high-minded academics, inspired artists or great athletes. We are meant to be free in ways we have no concept of, until the time comes when we awaken from all concepts to occupy that freedom directly.

As part of the process of inviting you to the threshold of many life-affirming insights, I will thoroughly explain *The 5th Phenomenon* as Awareness Field Theory, and frame it within a unique dimension of theoretical understanding. Many of the supporting ideas of AFT have been derived from a broad synthesis of multiple fields of inquiry such as physics, mysticism, philosophy and psychology. Specifically though, this work unfolds from my personal inquiry into, and direct experience of, the nature of consciousness itself. The axiom of direct experience is essential to this material—no matter how broad the academic or philosophical reach this examination achieves—because it is the *content* of the words that will, like the alchemists of old, speak intimately to the soul.

While *The 5th Phenomenon's* premise holds potentially groundbreaking insights for academia, it also speaks specifically to the reader, offering a window into the universal fields of awareness accessed directly by every human being. *The 5th Phenomenon* aids the individual by presenting an artful practice of depth consciousness, utilized for bridging subjective existence with the total bandwidth of Presence available to our sentience. This is how the world changes, one person at a time. Along the way, this work explores and challenges the scientific rationalism we so often feverishly pursue as empirical creatures. The relevancy of AFT insists that it is time for the cage of the human condition to be razed, as the era of psychology-based consciousness comes to a close.

## An Extraordinary Life

I invite you to consider that this examination can help move us all out of an existence dominated by fear and isolation, and into a life of clarity and freedom. I know it was possible for me. I also know that it is possible for others. So I am going to take you on a journey—one that may prove to be a pretty wild ride. We are going to cover some ground that I find few people talk about honestly. This book is designed to help bring depth to your seeing, which in turn can provide the inspiration to consciously and wisely choose the life you were designed to live.

One caveat before you proceed: This work will strip away the crutches we have all become accustomed to in our culture. Such inquiry will call upon the courage necessary to step outside of conventionally entrenched perceptions and personal coping mechanisms, and into the unpredictable wellspring of your own authentic existence.

The initial chapters deal with an academic approach intended to illuminate the structural aspects of consciousness for those in the fields of science. I invite you not to be intimidated or put off by any of it, for in the end we are all larger than words or ideas—there is genius inside all of us that often belies our own sense of possibility. I imagine us *all* exploring this together, because it is essential now for our species to get this subject out of the closet, and into the light where it belongs. Not to find what is right or what is wrong, but instead to discern what is *clear* for each of us—and to have faith that in the long view, all else will reconcile under the Intelligence of the Creator. ✲

# Chapter 3
# Introduction to Awareness Field Theory (AFT)

Without the phenomenon of awareness abiding in our human instrument as subjective consciousness, we would be inanimate objects, empty of the properties that quicken life. Science understands the body fairly extensively, but remarkably, has yet to establish a field of study around the phenomenon of sentience. Oddly enough, we must seek out the peculiar domain of spiritual mystics or perhaps philosophers to even begin to build a conversation around the perceptive qualities that illuminate the body. Those engaged in esoteric studies that are occupied with contemplating consciousness have often applied the terms *spirit* or *soul* to it, and the discussion inevitably becomes a mythological discourse. Of all the things in life that remain a mystery to us as human beings, it is curious to consider that something as intimate as our consciousness should be on that list. I would go further to suggest that it has become crucially significant to our evolution that the seat of our very existence should not continue to remain so wholly unexplained and unexplored by the general culture of mainstream knowledge. So this book begins with the most simple and obvious question: What is awareness?

To understand the complete picture regarding the qualities of human sentience specifically, it might be best to employ a bit of direct experience. Let us then start with the most direct and undeniable example of consciousness—your own. Consider a simple inquiry: What is this Presence within you that peers out at this moment through your eyes, taking in this page full of symbols? Actually feel into it for a moment, looking well beyond your association with *who* you think is looking out, to *what* you sense is looking out. What exactly is this phenomenon of perception you are presently immersed in? Could there be more happening in your experience at this moment than a mere scanning of symbols off a page by a biological brain that is interpreting them? I am going to suggest that there is more to you as a subject of consciousness than the neural-driven thoughts you swim in moment to moment. We are more than the mere machinations of a computer; more than a reduction of closed circuit intelligence reflexively processing data. Unlike artificial intelligence (AI), we are capable of sensing a field of awareness that is larger than the system of thought, and when we do, something magical happens. We become aware of consciousness itself; we become *self-aware*. To be more specific, we experience the localized sentience within us that animates thought, but at the same time we also become aware of an impersonal primary field of Awareness that animates consciousness itself—a Presence that exists and abides without our thoughts. This is the first step in sensing our capacity for *depth consciousness*.

# Introduction to Awareness Field Theory (AFT)

This simple exercise may seem relatively inconsequential to your thinking mind, but self-awareness is the miracle that sets us apart from most all living things, and because of it, we can live in intimate and direct association with our Creator. We retain the capacity to sense the ongoing merger of our individual consciousness with the inseparable Original Awareness from which we are sourced. There is an incredible import to this insight, because it suggests that we have access to an abiding Presence that is free of the mind, and all its associated thinking—good and bad. With this understanding, we are no longer bound to a reality dictated by the mere contrivances of the concept-bound psyche. Knowing this capacity to interface with a fuller range of consciousness than thought is the next step in our evolution. Without Presence appraising the human intellect, the mind would simply mirror the limited protocols of AI—and artificial intelligence can never qualify as "sentient" by AFT definitions, no matter how sophisticated the programming.

Sentience is often defined by science as the ability to feel or perceive—to have the capacity to *experience* subjectively. That definition would appropriately translate to every *living organism* on the planet, because all organisms relate to the environment around them in order to survive. All life has, to some degree, an ability to perceive the environment that it is immersed in—this is in fact the birthplace of subject/object relationship. But science virtually ignores the *phenomenon* of sentience, not recognizing its paramount significance. Science will refer to the perceptive ability of organisms over and over, never stopping to examine the nature and quality of perception itself. For many years I wondered why there had been no earnest academic inquiry around the subject of consciousness.

When the topic of AI emerged, I saw the problem more clearly. Science does not recognize sentience as a mystical endowment—therefore they equate the act of *perception* with that of simply *processing* information, which any computer can do.

Yet there is another more compelling reason for the neglect of this topic in scholarly circles. If empirical science were to inquire into the nature of consciousness, it would have to run the query through the standard existing models of dimensional references in the Universe for classification and analysis. With regard to analyzing this Presence within sentient activity, science would first attempt to qualify: Is it a force? Is it energy? Is it matter? Is it time/space? Or is it a quantum factor? I sense that the reason science has not delved into the subject of sentient awareness thoroughly is because consciousness itself does not fit into any of the aforementioned traditional systems of cosmological reference. Perhaps the major hindrance to an empirical review of consciousness is that awareness as a phenomenon is not directly quantifiable.

Yet I challenge any rational consensus that might suggest that we are incapable of even a rudimentary understanding of the dimension of awareness merely because such sentient fields cannot be classified within the standard working models with which we currently categorize the Universe. It is ironic to consider that the most intimate and direct aspect of being—our own field of conscious perception—has become, in my opinion, the most assiduously sidestepped subject matter in all of academia. As a consequence, the phenomenon of awareness has been routinely dismissed as some irreconcilable philosophical anomaly not worthy of rigorous examination. The empiricist's rejection of consciousness

# Introduction to Awareness Field Theory (AFT)

has for centuries now relegated ruminations on the matter to the obscure margins of mystics, philosophers and poets to decipher.

Prior to this book's exploration, consciousness has escaped a basic academic definition that moves any deeper than the occasional referencing of its observable characteristics. What makes this omission all the more astounding is that awareness may be (and I offer that it is) the only purely ubiquitous phenomenon in the entire universe. This fact should be of enormous scientific import. Yet how are we to embark on a direct examination of the actual nature of consciousness? With regard to awareness, one might ask, *how do we begin to approach the elephant in the room, when the elephant is the room itself?* Since we cannot currently fit the phenomenon of awareness into any known conceptual scientific framework, then it seems rather obvious that consciousness should warrant its own classification as a phenomenal dimension. This brings us to the subject matter of this book—*awareness as a legitimate phenomenon*, and to the new area of study I am introducing as Awareness Field Theory. Prior to the AFT approach, humans have only explored the nature of sentience with the tool of thought; but in *The 5$^{th}$ Phenomenon* we will explore the nature of consciousness with the very field of awareness it is sourced from, bringing our discovery to deeper levels of insight. With universal Presence as the fifth core dimensional element, Awareness Field Theory reveals a radically essential new order of functionality (*The 5$^{th}$ Phenomenon*), an operational element that completes and reconciles the currently recognized structural dimensions of the universe. Once this fifth dimensional reference is academically embraced, I predict that the supra-order application of AFT will shift scientific inquiry into a new era of discovery.

The following six chapters explore a mixture of established physics, systems theory, depth psychology, ontology, epigenetics, and my own AFT terminologies. I acknowledge that for many this can make for a somewhat dense reading experience. However, I find it necessary to lay down the framework of these concepts for academic exploration and application of AFT. For some, the intellectual understandings set forth in chapters 5 through 9 may be incidental, or even unnecessary to their own conducting of a path to clear consciousness, but for purposes of this book I find them relevant and essential. I have allowed for the possibility that many different mind-sets will be approaching the insights presented in *The 5th Phenomenon*, and the scientific world is an important part of that amalgam. Chapters 4, 5 and 6 are devoted to introducing the three phenomenal fields of awareness that make up the spectrum of Awareness Field Theory: *Noumenal Awareness (NA)*, *Quantum Field Presence (QFP)* and *Temporally Positioned Consciousness (TPC)*. These initial chapters—while tailored to suit the more scholarly readers—are introducing AFT terminologies and setting up the basic theoretical framework that the remainder of the book will often be referencing. ✺

# CHAPTER 4
## Noumenal Awareness

AFT commences with an exploration of the systems of awareness that make up the basic bandwidth of Presence throughout the universe. We begin with the primary Source Awareness from which two other phenomenal fields of Presence unfold. This original Source Awareness I refer to as *Noumenal Awareness (NA)*.

"Noumenal" is a word most associated with philosopher Immanuel Kant (1724-1804 CE) and his application of it. Kant used it to mean that which is not apprehensible by the senses, or even distinguishable by thought; which makes it an existence of sorts that is ultra-phenomenal, hence the term noumenal. Though Kant was not necessarily connotatively asserting it in the fashion I am here, the word *noumenal* has a nice fit for the purposes of providing some referential notion for that which ultimately cannot be named. Noumenal Awareness is something a physicist like Niels Bohr (1885-1962 CE) might label as an *ambiguous* aspect, because we may know it exists by virtue of its context, more than by its content—a phenomenon which we cannot locate in time or space to measure or examine directly. So we look to the context through which it arises, exists, or abides for clues as to its nature. Such is the mysterious quality of Noumenal Awareness; it challenges us as this original and eternal Presence that is both currently of, and prior to the Universe, and from which everything that ever was, or will be, emerges. Yet even as we consider the feature we are compelled to realize that there can be no object capable of penetrating the formless Noumenal realm, because all phenomenal objects exist only as a dimensional arising of Noumenal projections.

It is helpful to introduce a bit of ancient spiritual language to speak into these ineffable matters, because contemporary science, as I mention, has little to offer on the subject. Historically, the primordial aspects of AFT have been addressed by those willing to speak into the mystical qualities of existence. In many spiritual contexts, original awareness—that which exists prior to creation—is the *Godhead*, and given various names, such as "Brahman" for example, in the Vedic Hindu spiritual traditions. It is most always associated with the eternal and unchanging reality amidst and beyond the world, which cannot be defined, but can be *indirectly* known. I say "indirectly" because any actual sense of Brahman (God in this context) cannot arise from epistemic knowledge (knowing about something) since that Presence exists and abides prior to all states, and therefore is not a *thing* to know about. This beautiful existential quandary invokes an actual experience of it that orders on the sublime. Adi Shankara (788-820 CE), the father of Advaita Vedanta, extrapolates further by suggesting that because all things unfold

## Noumenal Awareness

from Brahman, and Brahman is unknowable, the only way to *realize* Brahman (Noumenal Awareness) is through an immediate and intimate *experience as an object of its creation*. It seems obvious to say that no point of consciousness can completely apprehend the Absolute from which it has unfolded, because it follows that nothing created can fully apprehend its Creator. We must allow for this sense of Noumenal Awareness as we invite science to arrive at some arrangement of scholarly humility that reconciles the ever mysterious, to the wonders of the known.

I predict that the possibility of us as a successful species is ultimately dependent upon an essential intimacy of human consciousness that is wedded to this non-state of *awareness-prior-to-objects*. Yet, how do we accomplish this union while we are simultaneously embodied as phenomenal objects in time and space? How do we marry the Noumenal (eternal) and temporal (mortal) natures within us? We possess aspects of the sublimely impersonal, lawlessly un-locatable, and fundamentally eternal, yet for the intellect, this is a mind-bending conundrum. The psychological koan this presents seems inevitable when we consider that our temporary embodiment cannot exist outside of (or separate from) the omniscient, omnipresent, and eternal Awareness of the Creator. Many personalities find these exotic aspects of our existence too difficult to reconcile, or even accept. We have become creatures of innate contradiction precisely because of this psychic dilemma. The paradoxical quality of our full nature has, in fact, been floating pools of philosophical thought for some time. Consider an excerpt from "An Essay on Man," a poem by Alexander Pope (1688-1744 CE) published in 1733 CE:

> *Placed on this isthmus of a middle state,*
> *A Being darkly wise, and rudely great:*
> *With too much knowledge for the Sceptic side,*
> *With too much weakness for the Stoic's pride,*
> *He hangs between; in doubt to act, or rest;*
> *In doubt to deem himself a God, or Beast;*
> *In doubt his mind or body to prefer;*
> *Born but to die, and reas'ning but to err;*
> *Alike in ignorance, his reason such,*
> *Whether he thinks too little, or too much;*
> *Chaos of Thought and Passion, all confus'd;*
> *Still by himself, abus'd or disabus'd;*
> *Created half to rise and half to fall;*
> *Great Lord of all things, yet a prey to all,*
> *Sole judge of truth, in endless error hurl'd;*
> *The glory, jest and riddle of the world.*

The very heart of the art of living lies in the holistic integration of these two seeming contradictions—the eternal and the temporal. As mythologist Joseph Campbell (1904-1987 CE) recognizes, the reconciling of these two aspects of our existence is "The Hero's Journey," and has been for all time.

Some may wonder how Noumenal Awareness could bear any significance in our lives if all we can do is have a concept about something that is beyond concepts. We have only to consider the limitations inherent in the core central doctrine of scientific inquiry: *If something is suggested that is not capable of being apprehended for empirical investigation, or defies certain known laws, it cannot be real*. From a purely rational point of view, one may consider just what the value in pursuing such abstractions might ever be. The answer to this question lies in the notion that the existence of Noumenal Awareness prompts us to the key psychological posture of *humility*.

It is essential that we humbly accept the primacy of the absolute field of Noumenal Awareness so that we may finally become fully transparent to it, thereby consciously feeling its influence. Indeed, it is within our organic design potential to artfully integrate a subjective openness to the fields of impersonal awareness, and the virtue of humility elicits it. This availability depends on a condition of surrender that carries with it no conceptual angle, no point of view and no motive. *A humble receptivity to the great unknown of our existence allows us to be available to the wisdom at the center of it.*

Feel the import of the statement in the preceding sentence somewhere inside you, in a place that does not rationalize it. In so doing we may become intimate with the very stillness that emanates from the ineffable Intelligence of the Creator itself. It is infusions of this infinite Intelligence that we are designed to bathe in consciously, and routinely, even as creatures moving in time and space. Individual access to original insight, creative inspiration or other conformation of intelligent intuition comes to us from this realm. Through humble surrender to the living mystery of the Creator, we touch into a transparency that organically moves us into alignment with a posture of absolute integrity to the Intelligent design of the universe. We will go into this axiom in greater detail, approaching it in many different ways, throughout *The 5th Phenomenon*.

Fundamental to embracing AFT academically is the basic tenant that the Noumenal Awareness realm in particular is of an anomalous dimension—beyond the ultimate singularity thresholds of our universe, and not accessible through the laws of classic relativity or even the reach of quantum mechanics. This mystery posits a frustrating obstacle for rational science, which has so far been unable to appraise us on the matter. Without rational science reconciling our sense of these subtle realms, the inevitable mythical hijacking of this unexplainable phenomenon has occurred. The subsequent naming of this sublime awareness attribute has, in fact, become notions of God. The act of labeling this mystery has been followed by the creation of various dogmas that coalesce into a pious fervor—creeds we have come to know through various contrivances of philosophical divinity and religious doctrine.

Yet the mystical aspects of creation offer more intimacy for human beings than mere belief. There is a beauty in embracing the unknown that can lead to epiphanies we had never anticipated. In order to facilitate this new order of understanding for science, I see the unknowable aspect of Noumenal Awareness as an invitation to regard it in the form of context, rather than content. Through considerations of context we can acquire some rational understanding of the place Noumenal Awareness occupies in our lives, and the Universe. The context in this case, presents itself as two specifically derivative fields of awareness that proceed forth from the Noumenal aspect. These precipitates reside within the realm of quantum mechanical reach, and classic relativity. They become the dimension in which we may begin to *touch* the untouchable. We will cover these two awareness fields (Quantum Field Presence, and

## Noumenal Awareness

Temporally Positioned Consciousness), which complete the basic bandwidth of universal Presence within Awareness Field Theory, in the following chapters.

It is predictable that most personality structures would shun mystery, which is why the majority of humans have chosen to build belief systems around the unknown aspects of our existence. Even when these systems of belief have historically led to distortion, separation and violence, much of our species still hold to them. The unceasing wars over matters of belief that have accompanied virtually every religious doctrine have historically caused some of the severest devastations ever wrought by our species. The academic approach to coping with the unknown too has its culpability. With its potential for intellectual arrogance and dogmatic rigidity, it exudes its own design of righteous aggression.

These destructive cycles demonstrate that there is little value in a purely intellectual posture or belief practice without a sustained integration of Noumenal Awareness to humble and illuminate it. Even the ideas detailed in this book are empty and pointless without this consideration of humility actualized. It is not prudent to continue to dismiss Noumenal Awareness as some nameless realm of reality as science and the prevalent social paradigms currently do—its aspect may be subtle, but its essence is the heart of life itself. As discussed earlier, even the phenomenon of our own consciousness has not found a scientific explanation within the traditional models currently accepted to define the classical universe. Amid the lack of academic embrace, we must refrain from the temptation to concretize pure awareness into stale notions of divinity, and build a religion or cult around it. We must heal the mind's innate anxiety regarding the prevailing uncertainty of this subject. Without such reconciliation the intellect is bound to perpetuate scholarly dismissal, or indulge the banal conversion of exquisite mystery to ecclesiastical myth. AFT offers direct insight to overcome all propensities to insulate ourselves from a naked rapport with the unknown so that we may find intimacy with it. ✪

# Chapter 5
# Quantum Field Presence (QFP)

The order of the cosmos dictates that there exists an undefined field of pre-form potential. Married to that pure condition of unrealized probability, particularized actualization occurs. This symbiotic dance of potential and manifestation is our universe in action. In the twentieth century, physics realized through probability theory, that there exists a background *quantum field* of possibility in *superposition* behind the singularly determined result we experience as our physical reality. This undetermined state arises from a dimensional facet of awareness that we qualify in Awareness Field Theory as Quantum Field Presence (QFP). QFP establishes itself as a precipitate of Noumenal Awareness. QFP functions as a subtle realm of Creator Intelligence, and one that harbors the master architectural and engineering design protocols that become the influencing genesis of our universe. This quantum ether looms just beyond the veil of our manifest universe—it is the precursor to all that is realized. It is the magic behind the ordinary, the mysterious behind the mundane, the lawless behind the ordered, and the unlimited possibilities behind the known distinctions of the cosmos. Separated from the systems of phenomena by a dimension threshold singularity, QFP simultaneously complements and abhors the myriad of closed systems that comprise the cosmos.

We have witnessed the almost century-long search to discover through phenomena, a Unified Field Theory (UFT) that reconciles the quantum and classical universe. This attempt has consistently fallen short because the actual unified field being sought by science is not limited to the content it unifies. With AFT, we can see that there is a unified field (Awareness) simultaneously permeating and transcending the contents of the universe. Scholars looking for a unifying factor within the contexts of forces, matter, energy or time-space, will always find that the search is doomed to yield consistently incomplete answers. AFT proposes that what physicists are actually seeking with regard to UFT transcends temporal projection. The missing integer sources itself from beyond our dimension—a pervasive Creator-generated Presence expressing itself through the various systems detailed in Awareness Field Theory.

When physicist Max Born (1882-1970 CE) first suggested in the 1920s that an electron's orbit could inexplicably *shift* from one position to another, he called it a "quantum leap." Because there was (and remains), no explanation for how or why an electron can relocate its orbit instantaneously without any measurable residue tracking how that transition took place, the action was labeled *quantum*. Viewed through the lens of AFT, we can see that the field of quantum mechanics emerges from the dimension of QFP. The awkward incompleteness within quantum theory today is unnecessary, and is reflected in the missing integer of *The 5th Phenomenon*—the dimensional fields of awareness that are currently not considered scientifically.

In modern physics there is an interesting tension between quantum theorists. The basic challenge arises around the anomaly of quantum lawlessness with the functions of classic Newtonian order. The breakdown in comprehensive understanding seems to occur at subatomic levels where the behavior of some particles, under certain circumstances, becomes inconsistent with the orders of relativity. In attempting to reconcile this anomaly, theorists produce a variety of postulates to wrangle some unifying explanation. The reigning notion is that quantum activity arises from within a closed system, a state of infinite probability that is in a micro-level superposition to mechanistic processes at the macro level. A particle in quantum realms would abide in a different aspect, a waveform state, because it is not fixed in a measurable position, or determined velocity. This theory is known as "wave-particle duality." Albert Einstein (1879-1955 CE) famously commented on the "difficulty" in reconciling the new theory relative to photons, but added, "We have two contradictory pictures of reality; separately neither of them fully explains the phenomena of light, but together they do."

In 1927 it was determined that quantum particles in superposition can be "collapsed" into a fixed place in phenomenon by observational intervention—by a human with a measuring device, for example. Science demonstrated and confirmed the end product of such processes, but curiously failed to consider the aspects of consciousness that initiate the collapse. This is science saying, *we believe in magic, but only with regard to the two card tricks we know about.* Academic minds simply overlook where the phenomenon of observer intervention in quantum reduction is pointing. AFT asserts that quantum systems and relative systems of order are completely complementary and correlative precisely because Presence is at once specific and non-specific. Quantum and relative systems at the level of awareness are orders that are inseparably enfolded, one into the other, functioning in phenomena as independent systems in symbiotic rapport. Science has not yet explored these factors because it does not recognize consciousness as a legitimate phenomenon.

I like to think of the biologist Charles Darwin's (1809-1882 CE) theory of evolution as the first truly quantum notion. Compromised by his claim that the construct of natural selection arises from the condition of *random mutation*—the convenient postulate seems as though it were likely calculated to avoid controversy. Seen from an AFT perspective, random mutation is hardly a coherent accounting of the profound occurrence of evolutionary processes. To Darwin's credit, there is boldness in the naturalist's assertion— especially for his time— that some performance-enhancing change (evolution) is occurring within organisms over generations—and holding to that contention, all while failing to provide precise and sound scientific explanations as to how or why. Darwin's theory of evolution persists today, and though it is still not comprehensively explainable by science, AFT addresses the matter succinctly.

Just exactly how did we come to mutate the miracle of an opposable thumb, or a higher foot arch with shorter toes, or a restructured, bowl-shaped pelvic girdle that supports upright locomotion? Were these very specific and intelligently designed adaptation components unfolded deliberately from the primordial Intelligence of the quantum field, or just some random genetic mutation that worked out really well? Darwin wouldn't allow himself to embrace or publicly promote Intelligent Design, so he chose the relatively peer-safe, but empirically questionable explanation of *random* mutation. AFT provides Darwinism with a theoretical crucible to unfold a comprehensive postulate on evolution.

The contemporary field of study known as epigenetics suggests that DNA evolves in a closed system, where all changes are tied to heritable factors. DNA regulations in the assemblage of repression, suppression, expression or mutation are all manifest from prescribed definitions that are supposed to be derived solely from ancestral origin. There are, however, exceptions. Not all covalent modifications of DNA in the conformation of chromatin remodeling are necessarily lineage-specific, just as not all genetic inheritance involves chromatic remodeling. Also, in the case of prions, we find proteins capable of inducing an infectious conformational state. These proteins are effectively presenting as epigenetic agents capable of catalytically prompting phenotypic change without a modification of the genome. These small examples are pointing toward the possibilities of genetic modification outside the machinations of heritable influences. AFT would suggest that Quantum Field Presence influences DNA evolution in a similarly non-lineage-specific way. This postulate elevates Darwin's random mutation theory by imbuing it with quantum qualities, and by recognizing a participatory Intelligence that is acting as an operational Presence to establish coherency to genetic change or adaptation. This is just an example of how QFP will begin to enhance and expand academic horizons within certain fields of study.

In summation, we see that QFP is surging with the operational mandate of the Noumenal realm, and that it exists as an unqualified field of Presence throughout the universe in a complementary dimension that is intimately wedded to, but fundamentally divergent of, the relativistic order of the temporally bound cosmos we perceive. The pervasively implicate fields of Awareness that permeate our universe demand their own epistemological category as part of the foundational framework within which the cosmos is structurally organized. Therefore, I suggest that prior to—and animating all of the four recognized elements of (1) time and space, (2) energy, (3) matter, and (4) force—is a seamless Creator-Presence I refer to in Awareness Field Theory as the yet unclassified $5^{th}$ *Phenomenon*. In short, consciousness is the fifth structural design element of the cosmos. This living awareness expresses through three basic formations: Noumenal Awareness (NA), which we have discussed in Chapter 4, Quantum Field Presence (QFP), which we are discussing in this chapter, and Temporally Positioned Consciousness (TPC), which we will discuss in the following chapter.

With the final addition of TPC we begin to see the entire bandwidth of Awareness Field Theory. Born from the womb of QFP's massive potentiality, the manifest cosmos is spewed forth as space, force, energy and matter. From its inception, the universe is imbued and sustained with the quickening of Quantum Field Presence as it passes through the Quantum Singularity Portal, differentiating into Temporally Positioned Consciousness—seamlessly imbuing the content of the entire cosmos. All manifestation is aglow with this primordial Intelligence, distilling down from Noumenal Awareness, collapsing through QFP and detailing out into the cosmos' various

## Quantum Field Presence (QFP)

aspects as TPC. The entire universe dangles from a thread of telescopically collapsed awareness field systems. In the realm of physics, what has been understood as the relationship between quantum mechanics and the classically mechanistic universe mirrors the relationship between what is described in Awareness Field Theory as Quantum Field Presence (QFP) and Temporally Positioned Consciousness (TPC) respectively. From AFT's perspective, every particle in creation is under the animating influence of Creator Presence, whether it is in a fixed measurable position or in the purported superposition of the waveform state. This is how Presence exhibits unified field properties. ✪

# CHAPTER 6
# Temporally Positioned Consciousness (TPC)

In time and space, Quantum Field Presence (QFP) collapses into the phenomenal matrix and abides there as Temporally Positioned Consciousness (TPC). Within the content of gravity waves, TPC exists as an unbroken awareness matrix. In inanimate matter, TPC abides as a fixed property, operating in coherence with that form's system of relative law. In the forces, TPC abides as an animating constituent of the cosmos. Where TPC inhabits life, the field of awareness expresses as *sentience* through an encapsulation of subjective consciousness that becomes assigned to a specific organism. The entire TPC field is pregnant with the Noumenal Intelligence of the Creator as it presses through quantum reductions. Within this system of Presence, any consequence is possible (the potential of the Creator ultimately abides without the constraint of law or lawlessness) within the dimensional realm of our universe. Though any possibility may be available, the awareness field system of our universe is designed to conform to distinct operational functions, and displays itself within the specific protocols of quantum collapse.

**Quantum Reduction**

*Vector collapse may manifest as an outcome of potential that is catalyzed by observer intervention through measurement;* this is a routine understanding in quantum physics. Physicist Werner Heisenberg's (1901-1976 CE) Uncertainty Principle explains that out of an infinite field of probability, we may locate a particle's position and determine its measurable characteristic attributes in space by observer intervention. This intervening act creates a reduction result (eigenstate) that has been selected (targeted) for by the observer from within the quantum field of probability. Temporally Positioned Consciousness, the field of awareness that I propose is contributing to this condition of collapse, curiously enough, is currently not a factor that is incorporated into any considerations as a qualitatively legitimate and integrated phenomenon in and of itself. *The 5$^{th}$ Phenomenon* suggests that Quantum Field Presence should become recognized and integrated as a fundamentally dimensional phenomenon in lieu of theoretical inquiries into the general study of physics and cosmology. Furthermore, its sister precipitate of Temporally Positioned Consciousness should likewise be assigned and incorporated as part of a mathematical language that addresses vector reduction from quantum fields into the manifold universe.

Academically accepted quantum theory describes aspects of quantum reduction quite specifically. The celebrated Austrian physicist Erwin Schrödinger (1887-1961 CE) has suggested that the quantum state is a kind of *continuous evolution* (expressed within

## Temporally Positioned Consciousness (TPC)

the Schrödinger equation). The initial projection of this waveform state, according to Schrödinger, is in a superposition, and is expressed as a non-invertible operation. For Schrödinger, superposition waveform probability is seen as a single quantum state that acts as an isolated system exhibiting no definite actualized result. However, Schrödinger's quantum state vision is confined only to an unbroken evolution of probabilities within that field, and therefore the elegance of Schrödinger's equation loses significant coherency at measurement intervention, and the subsequent conclusions of vector reduction. The supposition of the quantum realm as an isolated state degrades any considerations of calculating from the whole (AFT dismisses the existence of purely isolative states), and that fragmentation compromises the scope of his theory. Let me provide an example.

Waveform collapse that is catalyzed by measurement intervention (observation) is said by Schrödinger to be a reductive process that selects for a specific eigenstate, but AFT offers that this is only part of the picture. Awareness Field Theory brings to light a deeper context through which these dynamics can be viewed. When we see the Quantum system as a unique field of awareness (QFP), intimately wedded to other systems of awareness (TPC), we can then see how consciousness as a phenomenon is a legitimate factor of reduction. But before we clarify awareness field exchanges in quantum collapse, let me first offer a unique view of different models of reduction operating in our universe. What I am presenting for consideration in Awareness Field Theory is that there are at least two distinct expressions of quantum reduction inherent in probability outcome.

The first quality of reduction AFT introduces as a form of primordial, ephemeral matrix vector collapse. This movement establishes the cosmos by virtue of *creator impulse*. The act is not contingent on measurement or observational intervention to realize. AFT labels this kind of quantum collapse Inter-Cosmological Primordial Reduction Phenomenon (Inter-CPRP). The resulting phenomenal unfolding is not contingent upon observational intervention to catalyze its reduction (or concretize its actual existence by sentient apprehension). Subjective experience occurs after the manifestations of primordial reduction; therefore, the observer is not a factor of its collapse. Current quantum field theory recognizes the necessity for creation/annihilation operators, and Inter-CPRP in this scenario composes a coherent approach to making special relativity consistent with quantum mechanics. I maintain that the focus on Inter-CPRP as a creation operator within Awareness Field Theory can be a bridge to fresh unified field theory postulates.

The second, and currently recognized form of quantum collapse arises from perception-compelled waveform reductions, which we differentiate and refer to in AFT as Intra-Cosmological Awareness Vector Phenomenon (Intra-CAVP). Both demonstrate conditions of quantum reduction, but in the latter case of reductive intervention by observation, it is the influence of the observer's *directed consciousness* that compels *modified* outcome. The key differentiation that discerns sentient directed quantum collapse from Inter-CPRP, is that Intra-CAVP vectors form phenomena modifiers that catalyze through the interaction of consciousness fields as they transit intersecting Awareness Field vectors. Intra-CAVP reductions are actualized specifically from awareness systems mutually influencing

## Temporally Positioned Consciousness (TPC)

one another, and the full outcome of the exchange is *never* limited to just a specific eigenstate.

To summarize: The reductive influence of the observer intervention on quantum reduction lies not necessarily in the locus of any design, or specific focus of the intervening agent's intent, but that the collapse is primarily occurring under the direction of a purely mechanical component of mutually influencing AFT vector alchemies. These intersecting properties of consciousness are fulfilling complex design algorithm protocols as they engage in subtle, co-mingling awareness field exchanges. The interactions give rise to quantum-like expressions with particles, but this is only part of the outcome specific to consciousness features intersecting within AFT systems. Again, it must be emphasized that the full scope of Intra-Cosmological Awareness Vector Phenomenon (Intra-CAVP) reductive outcome is never limited to just eigenstate factors, but involve and include a broadly proliferate, and significantly more exotic product than is currently recognized or understood by quantum theorists. *The 5th Phenomenon* is pointing to these subtle, and as yet unknown formulations and asserting that it is time for modern physics to at least begin dialogue around the functions involved.

The nuances of AFT at this level of examination will include sublime operational distinctions at sub-micro levels of creation. Here we will discover that the complete picture is comprised of a lawlessly unbroken quantum awareness matrix acting as a crucible for TPC subset machinations in form—a paradoxical design detail that is both diverse and unified all at once. The difficulty for scientific inquiry will be that the *primary* reality feature of existence is open, unbroken, and immeasurable. As we look to the secondary apprehensible realities that unfold from the primary realm, we must avoid fixating solely on observable content just because of its empirical accessibility. Exploring *The 5th Phenomenon* means calculating from the whole (as abstruse as some aspects of it might be) and utilizing Awareness Field Theory as it embraces a full dimensional capacity for ambiguity.

**Directed Sentience and Incoherency At Vector Reduction**

Sentience abiding within living organisms is a relatively exotic form of cosmological consciousness. It is a type of embodied Presence that is itself aware, expressly of the environment around it, and is relating to the surrounding systems it is immersed in. Because sentience can direct its attention into other phenomenal fields, it has an influence on the objects of its focus. As we have said, these effects are a result of intersecting awareness field vectors, which are operating as a dynamic aspect of the creative equation of our cosmos. In this way, living sentience is functioning as an algorithmic co-determinant from within the epic history of the universe. Physics, as we have covered, has touched into the basic notion of *vector collapse,* or *quantum reduction,* but the operational property of awareness vectors as they display themselves in entanglement theory has yet to be discovered. (We will discuss consciousness vectors later in the book.)

The substance of our universe is designed and structured under the hallmark of a master design feature—a kind of sacred geometry of organically derived potentials at the Quantum Field Presence level. All unrealized quantum potentials within the field of probability are designed to reflect the coherency of this master design at actualization (Inter-CPRP manifestations). Under the direction of subsequent sentient-induced vector collapse via Intra-CAVP scenarios, the integrity of these orders are typically maintained, *unless* the subjective field of directed awareness catalyzing the reduction possesses incoherent vibration.

In our world it is only in the unique case of human sentience that we find vector reductions occurring under conditions of relative distortion. In such circumstances the quality and nature of human consciousness that is directing attention can contaminate the reductive product. These are instances where mendacious qualifications of human consciousness prompt a condition of *corrupted vector collapse*. This is how debased consciousness produces action or content that mutates sacred geometry, inflicting harmonic ruptures within the sound systems of creation—a malefactor we refer to in *The 5th Phenomenon* as violence. Violence, as defined by AFT, distorts the master design properties inherent in harmonic potentials, and poisons the wellspring of architectural beauty that permeates the universe.

Conversely, human actions undertaken by a conscious and coherent sentience find expression through a natural integration of their relationship to Source Intelligence. These are individuals who function routinely from Presence. Vector intervention initiated through such congruently aligned awareness will unfold *naturalized* results that maintain the integrity of the sacred geometry inherent within the structural orders of the universe. These organic reductions from the field of quantum potential are in harmonic accord because they preserve, express, and in some instances evolve the beauty of sacred geometry in those precise instances of reduction.

This inevitably prompts the question of whether there may be some representation of pre-determinism at play here. Does all this suggest that we are living in a universe that emphasizes a bias toward certain *favored* (harmonic) results, and actively does so by *preferring* outcomes congruent with sacred geometry? If we accept that the system of awareness selects for certain desired conclusions by *rewarding* coherent attention and intention with harmonic conclusions, we might not be able to escape the idea. Whatever the interpretation, it is safe to conclude that there is some kind of seemingly ordained equation on the part of the Creative Intelligence that produces reductions that are of a non-discordant nature under the influence of coherent observer awareness vectors.

**Singularity Thresholds**

As we have noted, the primordial essence of Noumenal Awareness births the precipitates of QFP and TPC, and the latter two arise as tandem and inter-related phenomenal systems. While the matrix of Quantum Field Presence remains as a fluid system of unbroken potential, the individuated aspects of Temporally Positioned Consciousness that descend into inanimate matter/energy and living organisms appear everywhere distinct. We may well be able to quantify aspects of the relationship between QFP and TPC without being able to reconcile the full and exact nature of one to the other. We must accept that pure Noumenal Awareness abides beyond the ultimate singularity threshold of apprehension, whereas the awareness field systems of TPC and QFP are confined to the phenomenal realms, and as such are subject to phenomenal study, examination and direct experience by sentient creatures. QFP and

## Temporally Positioned Consciousness (TPC)

TPC are themselves separated by a veil, a singularity threshold that functions as a subtle system boundary between the two. Singularities in AFT divide complementary dimensional systems that unfold from differing realms of phenomenal reality. These primary singularity thresholds I refer to as "portals." ✺

# CHAPTER 7
# Conversion Portals

Awareness Field Theory (AFT) has presented the two symbiotic phenomenal awareness systems that govern the reality we are immersed in. The first is QFP, operating from the quantum ether, and the second is TPC expressing as individuated consciousness within all matter, energy, space and force in the cosmos. AFT will now present four major singularity portals where our universe's dimensional veil becomes ruptured. Of significant scientific import is the insight that these thresholds are being trafficked by open awareness field systems. It is important that we explore these dimensional transition portals in order to more fully understand the role AFT occupies in contemporary cosmology, systems theory, and for future physics.

Portals are relevant to AFT because these dimensional veils are demonstrating the unbounded nature of open awareness systems as they operate through these unique conversion events. AFT embraces the ambiguous nature of Noumenal Awareness and its stunning omnipresence before, during, and after creation, but it is empirically essential that we recognize the trans-dimensional continuum of Creator Presence as it expresses in phenomenon through TPC and QFP. From AFT's subtle and inapprehensible abstractions, through to its contextual governing of Newtonian machinations, we will explore four pertinent singularity portals within which our universe becomes ephemerally transformed by awareness field systems transiting singularity. Here we may begin a coherent exploration of the operational fields of awareness within our universe, and our intimate relationship to the Intelligence that governs them.

**1) AXIS INVERSION PORTAL:** *Massive gravity fields (black holes) imposing time dilation ruptures.*

A time dilation point just inside the event horizon of a black hole's accretion disk obfuscates this singularity threshold. Here the inversion of the conventional *space-time* orientation converts to that of a *time-space*-based functionality in circumstances where massive gravity fields are pulling with such force that all matter under such influence achieves velocities approaching, matching and perhaps exceeding (tachyons, neutrinos etc.) the speed of light. Thus the point just inside the event horizon is where time-space, space-time dimensional axis inversion occurs, and perceivable phenomena presents the appearance of cessation from any one fixed point of reference. The effect on the relativistic observer is that in the former instance of *space-time functionality*, one looks into space and sees no time when arriving at any one point, and in the case of the latter *time-space functionality*, one looks through time at any one point and sees no spatial attributes; thus in the apparent *nothingness* of a black hole, and into that space beyond the event horizon of a black hole, "nothing" seems to occur.

"Something" *is* occurring, but it is occurring in another time (dimension) outside relative observer apprehension. The "blind spot," due to the axis inversion event inside the black hole at singularity, creates an *inter-cosmological relativity portal* that breaches dimensional ruptures of time dilation within TPC firewalls. AFT refers to this singularity threshold as the Axis Inversion Portal. What is actually happening beyond and within the event horizon of a black hole to the substances of our universe that enter therein is currently uncertain, and theories abound. What may very well be happening at the event horizon could be akin to a micro-scale version of a state approaching the pseudo-unified density condition of the GUT (Grand Unified Theory) era universe. The cosmological grist being crushed inside a black hole could be so significant that the *weight* of it, though unseen, is contributing to the overall gravitational expression in the universe we observe. This may be a partial aspect of the so-called missing mass in the universe that cosmologists say is the lost variable in expansion rate calculations of the cosmos. Infinite density scenarios relative to QFP/TPC conversion will be further discussed when we cover the *Infinity Portal*.

The significance of the Axis Inversion Portal for Awareness Field Theory will be determining whether TPC assignments are reestablished, evolved or dispersed at this portal's singularity threshold. If substance is somehow mutated at singularity, then TPC would remain as an affiliated awareness precipitate, but it would express as a transformed consciousness factor of the new *product*. In such scenarios a Quantum Field Presence that harbors the architectural blueprint of the new dimension or exotic realm would govern the transfigured substance. It remains to be discovered whether or not QFP is an indivisible governing component for all realms and realities (omnes ratio), or whether QFP exists in as many multiple arrangements (multis aspectus) as there are dimensions or universes to govern. The Axis Inversion Portal reveals insight into how QFP is responding to the imposition or introduction of new orders of substance through human modifications of genetic material, and how AFT entanglement functions express themselves through singularity features.

## 2) THE INFINITY PORTAL: *Pre-Planck epoch universe point of origin, occurring at infinite density.*

The Infinity Portal singularity is the threshold of universal origin, and involves the crunch of space-time as we look back through temporal dimensionality. This embryonic phase of the cosmos is understood as the "pre-Planck epoch" of our universe at infinite density. This portal presents a time-dilation singularity trait when viewed from any relative observer's point of reference, so no possibility of observer apprehension is available—or ever will be. Most notable is the theoretical supposition that infinite density retains a non-structural theme that ultimately defies any space that would allow for the occupation and function of relativity, or of its complementary quantum states. Beyond this threshold all laws of the observable universe no longer apply—because they no longer exist. The Infinity Portal also divides the birth/destruction cycles of the phenomenal awareness field realms. Dimensional annihilation at this singularity is whole-scale, displacing even QFP functions in superposition.

## Conversion Portals

Through infinite density conditions, all is transformed to a non-specific state of *receptivity*. The pre-Planck epoch universe will remain in an abiding posture of pure responsiveness to Creator impulse, as it awaits the next era of conception. This is an existence without design, and AFT refers to it as the Infinity Portal. At this singularity, TPC and QFP will become *fused* into a kind of unity consciousness, awaiting re-birth, and a new allocation of assignments when the cosmos will once again be reborn and restructured into a new order of diversity and expression.

**3) QUANTUM PORTAL:** *Quantum conversion entanglement expressing as dark matter.*

The Quantum Portal is a theoretical AFT singularity threshold that reveals to us that the massive fields of surging potential looming just behind the QFP/TPC conversion veil are physically influencing the universe. The relationship between Quantum Field Presence and Temporally Positioned Consciousness is intimate and unique, and predicated on the sublime correlative of entanglement, which theoretical physics recognizes but cannot explain. AFT offers essential insight into entangled systems with regard to the ongoing rapport of awareness field vectoring and exchange. The singularity details of this portal will also address relational TPC/QFP conversion issues surrounding the expression of genetically engineered modification scenarios, organ tissues transplants, cloning, and the prospect of any pending successful cryogenic procedures attempting to achieve the milestone of suspended animation. The governing dynamics of QFP infusion also serve to expose the myth that artificial intelligence can become self-aware.

An examination of the Quantum Portal through the lens of AFT is best served by a discussion around what cosmology and physics refer to as dark matter. These are instances of an apparent mass-induced gravitational influence on the fabric of time-space, but with no apprehended mass known to exist that might create such gravitational effects. AFT suggests that the bulk of this phenomenon is not due to invisible matter we cannot detect, but is a display that results from the conversion factors of Quantum Field Presence (QFP) to Temporally Positioned Consciousness (TPC) within the inter-cosmological vector collapse (Inter-CPRP) that creates the universe we observe. The gravitational presentations are pointing to AFT mechanics involving gravity function calculations that are not mass related, but conversion tension derived.

Our entire cosmos is a result of an induced (and sustained) reduction state of TPC, sourcing from the preemptive QFP flux. The unexplainable gravitational effect we observe is pointing to a fifth order (AFT) function—one that is generating the fourth order product theorized to be dark matter displays. Dark matter phenomena appear to increase gravitational force exponentially when occurring around greater concentrations of galaxy clusters (matter). The exponentially high value gravitational footprint is due to AFT exchange vectors between QFP and TPC that are being extrapolated from AFT *entanglement scenarios*. The matrix of QFP, through the act of TPC infusion into matter, presents a conversion *tension* through entanglement that creates the gravitational signature that is speculated to be due to invisible matter.

Inside the cosmos, QFP-to-gravity wave (time-space matrix) vector reduction scenarios involve a subtler and more diffuse tension

## Conversion Portals

than do QFP-to-matter infusions. As such, the differing value and nature of the conversion dynamics between matter and gravity waves (space) result in influences that are not proportionate—and which do not equalize or offset. The imbalance and qualitative contrast of conversion tension reveals an effect that exhibits a presentation similar to the influence of mass on the fabric of time-space. Science at some point will come to the realization that gravity should really be characterized as more of a pseudo-force. AFT sees gravity as a phenomenon derived from context (as in gravity waves *inflate space*), and therefore it is of a qualitatively different nature than that of the other recognized forces (electromagnetic, nuclear, strong and weak) proper. The weak coupling constant, lack of an associated particle, and the singularly attractive nature of gravity testify to its esoteric properties, and QFP/TPC conversion to gravity wave exchange is similarly unique.

QFP/TPC conversion operations reveal that awareness systems fundamentally breach the singularity of inter-realm portals, effectively occupying two or more dimensional systems at once. Because of this we are able to observe phenomenal effects of Awareness through classically mechanical displays of gravitational influence on objects in time and space due to the profound QFP/TPC conversion influence of awareness field systems vectoring such portal thresholds. It must also be noted that QFP/TPC entanglement functions vary relative to the reductive essence or property that QFP is collapsing into. These variations are what express differing degrees of tension that present as "weight" in gravitational realms, like the one our cosmos is seated within. This factor also addresses the controversial notion that the human soul may have a "weight" of 21 grams—more or less.

The Quantum Portal is an awareness field singularity transit that is actively exhibiting observable effects we can measure, and not just in quantum probability functions. Of primary significance is the fact that we can no longer take for granted the significant co-factors of Awareness Field Theory that give rise to these phenomena. At some point science will reconcile many intangibles of *The 5th Phenomenon*, but new mathematics will most likely be needed. The complementary nature of the awareness field derivatives of QFP and TPC will likely require exotic arithmetic to reconcile.

**4) ENTROPIC COLLAPSE PORTAL:** *Total entropic exhaustion of the Universe ending with inertia sublimation.*

At the very margins of the known universe, time and space finally yield to a state of entropic collapse as the mechanical systems of the cosmos unwind from the last spasms of the structural tensions that energized them from the birth of creation. At this point, gravity waves themselves cease to inflate space, and by extension, time. The singularity factor here is an annihilation operator, where all residual momentum of the expanding cosmos edges to a standstill; it is where our universe ends and non-dimension begins. Far, far out in the nether reaches of space, the sublime nature of entropic collapse creates a random distortion of the classical mechanics that have driven the gears of creation through the cosmos from the beginning of time. Here the dying universe is giving rise to the thermodynamic degradation that devolves into a radical disorder, a chaos that will ultimately settle into a uniform inertia that becomes the Entropic Collapse Portal at the very edge of our universe.

## Conversion Portals

Expressing itself as an absolute inversion of the infinite density singularity, the Entropic Sublimation Portal is a zero-sum entropy threshold that ultimately prompts the massive dimension of our cosmos to finally yield to the non-dimension of the void. The end begins not with a bang or a whimper, but through the passive veil of an inductive time-dilation property that negates any empirical apprehension of this apocalyptic margin by the relativistic observer. The colossus of churning order we call the cosmos has finally played itself out to a placid sublimation where space-time quietly ceases to impress the void.

TPC in this chaos realm undergoes a transformation from the system order of the classic universe to the random de-evolution scenarios of entropic sublimation. QFP/TPC conversion thresholds are dissolved, and the quantum field no longer operates as a system in superposition to realized phenomena. The continuous evolution of infinite probability capacities within the quantum realm are no longer maintained as a non-invertible operation, and the quantum field degrades and implodes into a uniform reduction of random chaos that merges with phenomena, becoming a singular lawless content within the entire entropic collapse. The Entropic Sublimation Portal initiates the scenario of QFP/TPC merging, where the two systems collapse into one another, making phenomena, and all related order, a capricious dimension in its death throes.

Eventually the entire cosmos will be assimilated by the gradual degradation of entropic sublimation, beginning at the margins of the universe and collapsing inward; ultimately, back to the original point of infinite density that existed just prior to the "Big Bang," where the whole process repeats itself for another cycle. Like a massive inhale and exhale, this is the death and rebirth of the cosmos that Hindu mythology calls the Day and Night of Brahma. In the cosmic cataclysm of this final scenario, Quantum Field Presence and Temporally Positioned Consciousness are devoured as systems by chaos, ultimately merging into infinite density at the nadir point of entropic collapse. Through it all, Noumenal Awareness yet abides—ever present, eternal and unchanged.

As exotic as these cosmological proposals may seem to be, they are important, even if only to detail that it is essential that we begin to build a discussion around AFT dynamics as they relate to the workings of the universe at large, and not just relegate our examination of awareness fields to personal consciousness. I find it exciting to sense into the potentials for exponentially expanding our understanding of the total reality we occupy. There is a key premise espoused in Awareness Field Theory—that *fundamental awareness is not confined to any one singular design attribute, dimension or realm of the universe.* This chapter on conversion portals provides just a beginning sense of what possible explorations into AFT might offer relative to physics and cosmology. ✦

# CHAPTER 8
# Systems

A look at systems theory is essential to an understanding of the operational aspects of AFT because systems exist everywhere. There are systems within human social landscapes that include political, economic, cultural and technological systems, just to name a few. Within nature there are ecosystems, climate systems, tectonic systems, oceanic systems, and the cosmological system of our universe. Awareness too has its systems.

There are two basic types of systems that AFT recognizes—open systems and closed systems. With regard to those systems, AFT offers an enhanced definition that is somewhat different than that of classic physics or traditional mathematics.

Closed systems in AFT are defined as features with boundary that possess relatively consistent qualitative and quantitative content at any given moment (mass or energy exchange is not a factor). Open systems in AFT by contrast do not have fixed properties, nor do they have *locatable* boundaries, but they do exhibit characteristics in contexts that denote an operational cohesion while influencing closed systems. The content of an open system however, defies determination. Measurement of open systems is arbitrary because the value of an open system is known only by virtue of how it affects the content and operations of the distinct closed system it is interacting with. There are only two purely open systems in our universe, and they are both systems of awareness. The recognized open systems in AFT are Quantum Field Presence, and Temporally Positioned Consciousness. In the mysterious ethers of probability potential, the open system of QFP surges with Creator Intelligence. In the cosmological matrix of our manifest universe, the open system of TPC infuses the entire universe with Presence.

Creation itself is an amalgam of mutually interfacing closed systems. AFT asserts that all systems are successful in perpetuating themselves because their design is effective at establishing an *existential persistence*. Successful systems do not fall under the absolute control of local systems they encounter. In the inverse, they do not operate in an absolute vacuum unaffected by other systems (*isolated systems are a fallacy, and do not actually exist*). Systems are engineered to co-exist in a symbiotic rapport that achieves mutually radical homeostasis, free of absolute external regulation, or hampering influences from other systems. There is a clear intelligence in the scheme of the ordered processes that fixed systems demonstrate.

Yet there is a curious and marked exception to the rule of coherent design directives within closed systems. It turns out that a human being's psychological capacity for self-awareness has resulted in a characteristic that can deviate from the harmonic system expression of consciousness. The seriousness of this anomaly means we are left to reconcile this functional peculiarity, or perhaps prematurely impose extinction upon ourselves because of the gravity of the incongruity. Awareness Field Theory addresses the misguided pretext that arises due to the fragmenting capacities of the self-reflective psychic system of our species. Yet even amid such considerations, we accept that this malapropos variance is part of the overall design feature of a radically free sentience that possesses near infinite possibility. The Creator is not a regime of totalitarian benevolence. Chaos must find its own coherency.

With regard to systems specifically, the notion of *chaos* becomes another one of those ideas that requires a more useful characterization. AFT defines chaos as a condition whereby the protocols of any closed system emphasize random possibility over ordered conclusions. Chaos systems utilize seamless exposure to impersonal awareness Intelligence in order to extract fluid coherency of expression amid a multitude of unpredictable factors. Creator Intelligence influences these complex calculations of random probability by actualizing harmonic moment-to-moment results from the radically open field of possibility. Such operations induce fluid responses within closed systems that express physically in ways that resemble the flow of water, or a swarm of bees. There is a necessity for randomness in these systems that manifests as a form of order that is not predictable, but neither are these systems exhibiting a non-functional chaos. Harmonic chaos does not express destructive or incoherent themes. The open systems of QFP and TPC continuously wed chaos with coherency to produce organically harmonic results in phenomena.

Chaos systems conform to the governing of Creator Intelligence through a nearly infinite field of possible action. This functionality is designed to successfully facilitate a spontaneous and immediate adaptation to a myriad of variables being encountered in any one moment. Nobel Prize winning American mathematician John Nash Jr. (1928-2015 CE) applied mathematical applications to complex systems in order to approach nonlinear operations with some sense of coherency in game theory, but the approach is predicated on mapping subject intent derived from noted human motivational factors. Within AFT, we see pure chaos as an adaptive trait that is designed to deliver immediate and fluid response to circumstances presenting near infinite variables. In the natural order, some environments or circumstances necessitate that chaos protocols reign supreme as the prime functional directive of the system. For example, the immune system is not a chaos system because it is designed for a defined response to very specific circumstances, targeting for a distinct result. But that kind of response protocol is not efficient to conduct a herd of gazelle in flight from a predator over random terrain. Interestingly enough, the human mind when in organic spontaneous reflex conducts itself with chaos system idiosyncrasy—an operational quality of the same order that would govern stampeding buffalo. But that spontaneous process can also be subject to degeneration from the linear imposition of conceptual abstraction, which reduces the radical fluidity of chaos potentials to a cumbersomely predictable element that is seeking control or specific results within defined parameters.

Ascertaining predictability may be the holy grail of all scientific inquiry, but it is also the slippery slope of thought-based consciousness because the effort necessitates the arrangement of theoretically compartmentalized control machinations onto organically whole system landscapes. For example, Nash Equilibrium Theory finds a window of application in certain areas of focus within complex systems such as economics or war game scenarios, yet it simultaneously defines its own fragmentation by reducing the system of thought to a rational decision-making protocol influenced by motivation derived from contexts of conflict and cooperation. Over and over we find brilliant academic minds rendering elegant observations by obfuscating the full presentation of order, so as to acquire some variable of niche control. The academic strategy for engaging selective discernment can be useful in determining relative predictability for specific venues, but we must not forgo the knowledge that the theoretical movement sacrifices considerations around critical elements of the whole. This failure to calculate *from* the whole comes about primarily because the isolated intellect abhors analyzing variables of the equation that represent the more ambiguous aspects of order. While such focused problem-solving has its utilitarian place, the human mind is certainly not designed to live out of this computational protocol by attempting to use it as a mode of operation for the overall expression of sentience. In selecting for rationalization over other dimensions of consciousness, we entreat pathological compartmentalization of the psyche, which in turn invokes a sense of isolation from Presence. This is *the* error we find rampant in the human condition today.

    The most intimate exploration of clarity for individual consciousness occurs through the cultivation of open system impersonal awareness features influencing the complex closed system of the thinking mind. Pure Presence is complementary to personal sentience, and is intended to govern subjective consciousness through the lifetime of its physiological journey by informing the chaos of human thought through the sublime algorithmic influences of primordial Intelligence. The mind's organic design provides a capacity that allows for lucid access to where Creator luminescence abides. This transparency to pristine awareness fields is critical to the prevention of the human mind's propensity toward isolation and psychic distortion. It is a profound realization when we come to understand clearly that violence in humans *always* occurs when the system of thought is functioning as if it were a remote operation, practicing an intended disassociation from Presence.

When operating in such rogue fashion, the subjective mind will routinely attempt to take personal ownership of any transpersonal inspiration or creativity that descends organically into the human mind—dismissing the essential realms that saturate the psyche with insight. The intellect as a system, without Presence nourishing it, will habitually seek to dominate the environment it is interfacing with. Human beings, while operating solely out of thought system consciousness, seem routinely drawn to control and exploit free systems—and nature was our first target. History shows that in addition to natural environments, systems of creative human enterprise eventually also become grist for the tyrant's mill.

The first historically significant authoritative abuse of human innovation was that of agriculture. We have built empires on grain, mutating it into an industry of food production. Through the creative insight of pulverizing the responsive life-giving fertility of seed into an inert consumable flour to feed the masses, select individuals have become empowered by owning and controlling the commerce. Consider also the early technology of the Gutenberg printing press in 1440 CE, the first non-essential machinery to serve the masses at large. By 1482 CE, this system of information gathering and dissemination became monopolized in the European theater by The Roman Catholic Church. The Church, by extension, also installed the first monopoly on the institutions of education that utilize books—another application of controlled tyranny levied against a technology of free-system potential.

Current economic systems reflect this cold standard. A list of the inspired victims of ego tyranny, as you might imagine, emerges in all areas of creative enterprise—from genetic engineering to music and film.

When interfacing with free system landscapes, we must rely on our innate availability to the full dimension of awareness fields to illuminate our participation in the orders we are attempting to interface with. Ultimately, the relationship with radically free chaos is ours to reconcile, but we can never reach that place by imposing corrupt agenda-driven control and regulation over free systems any more than we can attain so-called "enlightenment" through directed thought. The regimes of war or revolt, writer Ralph Waldo Emerson (1803-1882 CE) observed, did not truly abolish slavery; it ended ultimately "...through the repentance of the tyrant." Chinese philosopher Lao-Tzu (604-531 BCE) refers to this self-regulated harmonization arising out of a radically free state of system chaos as *tzu-jan*, emerging in and of itself, without external imposition or compulsion. The wisdom of tzu-jan harmony is not predicated on subjective volition. Even so, fragmented thought consciousness continues to press for its desired result of control as a variable of system chaos inside the mind's functioning.

## The 5th Phenomenon

Within Awareness Field Theory, creativity and inspiration are recognized as a necessary chaos; a system of random probability potential meant to be influenced by original Presence. Yet personal thought structures often impede the natural transmission of awareness fields that harbor Creator Intelligence, denying access to the very realm that would permeate and guide the free state of conceptual consciousness. This error prompts a dangerous condition given the potent technological advances we have pursued in the last one hundred years. If we fail to integrate a lucidity of presence that enlightens the radical systems of thought, we will continue to suffer the tyranny of renegade psyches that often become imposed one against another. We see that this is distortion. We see that this is violence. We see that this is the root cause of war and of all inorganic expressions of destruction. The depths of awareness are ever available to still the waters of thought's chaos, but we must learn to cultivate access to them.

Returning again to Lao-Tzu, and chapter 2 of the Tao-Te Ching, the notion of *hsiang sheng*, addresses the concept of the systems of the universe (nature) emerging as a mutual arising. One system's "way" moves in absolute freedom, but is inseparable from every other system of the universe, which also moves in its own "way." These systems will harmonize organically if left open to Presence, and not forced by unnatural imposition into some contrivance of artificial order. The only thing capable of that kind of tyranny (artificial order) is the rogue paradigm of conceptual thought. The unripe self-reflexive mind of humankind eschews the openly fluid and reconditely responsive systems of free-form awareness that are known in the Tao Te Ching as *hsuan*. Severed thought peers out from under the rock of its imagined existence, points its finger in horror at that which mystically arises and inexplicably unfolds, and labels it "chaos." That terrifying mystery is, in fact, the manifestation and order of primordial Presence. What the Ego perceives as overwhelming is actually our true home. It seems almost absurd to consider that the Intelligence that dreamed us into fruition could appear so frightening to the psyche.

A later Chinese philosopher, Chuang-Tze (370-287 BCE), puts it this way, from the *Zhuangzi*: "The Order of the Tao is not law, it is *wu-tse* (non-law)." The operations of the Creator as expressed through awareness field systems (animating the Tao) are dimensionally sublime—far too subtle—and possessed of too many intangibles to ever be completely apprehended by ruminations of the isolated psychic structure. Its expression is evidence of its order in action. The Tao of creation must be allowed to flow like the water, coalesce and dissipate as the clouds, and settle in random fashion as grains of sand on the beach. The Tao represents all systems, and Awareness Field Theory confirms and explicates those functions.

The fields of awareness presented in AFT are complementary systems that will not reconcile separately; reconciliation only occurs when AFT systems are taken as a whole. For the system mechanism of rational thought to attempt to partition itself from Creator Presence is a violation of the organic order of the Tao. Manifesting distinction from unity is the sole domain of the Creator. Reverse engineering the Creator is an act of arrogance. Such division of consciousness becomes the incubator of violence. Conceptually compartmentalizing existence into isolated programs of operation without due consideration of the whole has been the fundamental error of the human mind's reflection on the nature of reality.

# The 5th Phenomenon

An operational definition of human sentience limited to the brain (or any closed system) would not be capable of reconciling the following koan-like statement from celebrated physicist Neils Bohr (1885-1962 CE): "The opposite of a correct statement is an incorrect statement. The opposite of an absolute truth, is another absolute truth." Or as I sometimes say, *always, there are no absolute truths*. These assertions invite considerations of another order that would transcend a merely reasonable answer to ascertain worthwhile meaning. Likewise, a full understanding of existence is not to be derived solely from calculations rendered from the box of thought. We are immersed in fluid fields of awareness, subtle systems that imbue us with insight, intuition, stillness, inspiration and creative epiphany; we must discover an artful integration of those awareness systems in order to function according to our full organic design.

If the nourishing influence of impersonal awareness sourced from Being were a commodity, it would be the most precious resource in all of creation. How we utilize our access to it determines the quality of our existence. As such, it becomes necessary to consider a relationship to the full depth of consciousness that animates our life. Yet too often the taintless field of Presence that nurtures human sentience is encumbered with routine discharges of distorted thinking; a process that is the precursor to all unconscious conduct in the world. This smog of unenlightened action dulls and reduces our visibility individually, and as a society in general.

Broken thought has become a landfill where we choose to let our children play. Splintered awareness has become a cesspool from which families have chosen to drink water. Fractured consciousness that is disassociated from Presence has become a smoke stack from which society continues to breathe. We must endeavor not to live out of the realms of the disjoined psyche, or we will experience large-scale destruction of the very habitat that sustains us. We have a responsibility to honor and utilize the full systems of awareness that quicken our bodies as living creatures, and in so doing discover the balance of their design protocols. We have continued to allow our minds to run amok without restraint or even a due consideration for the folly we perpetuate every day by indulging a consciousness that is not rooted in the stillness of Being. Consider the following AFT creed, crafted for inspiration:

### The Awareness Preservation Project

- *We perceive the general field of human awareness as a natural, open space habitat, designed for the utilization of healthy conscious expression.*

- *We perceive that the encroachment of unregulated conceptual development onto the organic environment of human awareness fields is a dangerous misuse of natural resources.*

- *We perceive that any healthy conceptual development respects and preserves the vast expanse of wild awareness only through integration with it.*

- *We perceive that a conservation of sentience means the prevention of exploitation and depletion of vital human awareness resources.*

- *We perceive that fixing attention only, or even mostly, on developed conceptual paradigms without routine and significant immersion into open-space wild awareness creates a toxicity of consciousness.*

What would happen if we began to routinely seat our attention in a place larger than the human intellect, immersing our sentience into the fluid field of open awareness that bathes us in the very Intelligence that creates and governs the universe? What if we evolved a protocol of consciousness that shifts us away from conceptual knowledge as the primary directing factor of our perceptions? What if we became so settled in the craft of full Presence that we could maintain a continuing transparent access (from our minds and bodies) into transcendent realms that animate and inform our lives and actions? What *would* actually happen is nothing short of the end of all violence. Let us move deeply into the subtle, wild and intuitive operational dimensions of awareness now, and end the sad legacy of the sundered human existence that our ancestors labored under.

When I was in college, a philosophy professor once told me my interpretation of a Plato (427-347 BCE) dialogue was wrong. Wrong? "I thought this was a philosophy class," I said. "Yes, it's my philosophy class. And you're wrong," he replied. If we both had armies (and had I an interest), perhaps we could have fought over who was "right"—me the young radical with new ideas, and him the old-guard, established regime of authority. This is what happens when Being becomes walled off by an intruding intellect that claims to know what is right and what is wrong. We no longer have a creative intercourse of relational exchange; we have instead ideological and literal war. Case in point: Human history. We must utilize the system of awareness in the way that it is designed to operate, or the successive and routine experience of polarization leading to conflict will be inevitable. ✪

## Chapter 9
## Human Sentience

When Temporally Positioned Consciousness (TPC) abides in matter giving rise to living organisms, it expresses itself then as sentience. Academic discussions on the general topic of human sentience inevitably end up centering on some notion of "intelligence." The premise of such dialectic is holding to the belief that awareness is solely limited to the narrow operational bandwidth of the intellect. Intelligence in these examinations is often defined as the capacity to receive and process information. This is the typically mechanistic reduction of working consciousness that one finds in scientific inquiry where Cartesian (philosopher Rene Descartes 1596-1650 CE) points of view reign supreme. Yet, this perception of consciousness is so narrow that it is by definition capable of including artificial intelligence into the realm of sentience. The notion that the full dimension of human awareness is merely a result of our receiving, interpreting, and processing data through our senses is clearly too limiting to be either accurate or useful. Such assertions also infer that this model of human consciousness as a system, like that of artificial intelligence, must be a closed one.

But is it true that consciousness is a closed system? AFT would posit that the full field of conscious awareness is not confined to the limited order and operation of closed systems. In the specific case of humans, faculties of intuition, original insight, creative inspiration, instinct, and a host of other nuanced, brain-transcendent features present themselves daily in our lives as absolute anomalies to the closed system theories of human intelligence as consciousness. Consciousness must be—and is—more than the mechanistic reductions of unambiguous psychic protocols and the physiological properties that drive them. Awareness Field Theory integrates into the notion of consciousness the ambiguous aspects of Presence moving within subtle dimensions. These are awareness fields that animate the physical brain but are not confined to the physical brain. AFT models of sentience declare that impersonal awareness fields interface moment to moment with our existence, just as they do with all aspects of the manifest universe.

The complete order of consciousness in humans involves more than an *experiencer*—more than the mere *subject* of awareness. To fully engage the entire bandwidth of our dimensional Presence moves us beyond psychic structures, even if not transcendently so. We are looking at unfolding and enfolding systems of awareness that are involved. With AFT, we are considering the cascade of awareness fields, from primordial Noumenal Awareness to Quantum Field Presence, on down through Temporally Positioned Consciousness when we examine the animation of the body-mind.

How a field of awareness specifically illuminates the body is, curiously, not a common academic topic—most approaches utilize some form of religious elucidation. The expositions typically involve an ecclesiastical notion of a spirit that endows the body with the "spark of life." With *The 5th Phenomenon,* we are looking to a clarity on the subject that is arrived at through direct experience more than we are looking toward conjured myth for belief or faith acquisitions. AFT offers for consideration the two distinct awareness features of QFP and TPC as the primary fields that constitute the system of human sentience. The specific complementary quickening aspects of these realms are described in AFT as *Being* and *Monad*, respectively.

*Being* is the open field of impersonal awareness that is married to all individuation in the universe. It is alive with the Intelligence of the Creator. It is not "of this world" (as Jesus might say) by origin, or limited to it in operational scope. Being participates intimately as an active agent of creation and annihilation, because Being derives its animation from its association with Quantum Field Presence (QFP). Being is often overlooked by the psychic paradigm of human consciousness, even though we are designed to access Being directly in order to align with the flow and art of coherent expression. Being may come to be revealed in many ways. Rumination, contemplation and meditation are often suggested as portals to Being, mostly because these activities are often associated with the liberation of attention from thought. But these aforementioned methods are not the only way to access Being, and in my own case not even the most effective. Surrender (discussed in Chapter 20), I found to be the most profound route to Being, and Love (discussed in Chapter 15) the most direct.

*Monad* is a more specific element than Being. By AFT definition, Monad is a discreet feature of Presence that is attached to living organisms, and is most commonly referred to in the world vernacular as a "soul." Within Awareness Field Theory, we prefer the word Monad to soul. The word "Monad" connotes significantly less religious and mythological residue than do the words "soul" or "spirit." Monad is essentially the embodiment TPC undertakes when animating life. Monad, within the context of AFT suggests an encapsulation of awareness that carries an associative relationship with something beyond itself. To this end, "Being" interfaces with subjective sentience through the Monad's affiliation of consciousness assigned to living systems. Monad is a correlative aspect to the field of Temporally Positioned Consciousness (TPC), forming a structural association that binds itself to a distinct living entity.

The Monad in turn quickens three somatic regions of sentience in the human body through its allocation of TPC. Those three physiological subsets are comprised of the traditionally recognized Id and Ego, with an additional AFT attribute included that is referenced as the *Vig*. These three qualities retain corporeal affiliations in the body at the root chakra (Id), the heart chakra (Ego), and the crown chakra (Vig), respectively. The human experience of sentience is structurally animated by this trifecta of the Id, the Ego, and the Vig. These centers inform the human instrument in three ways: Through DNA encoding via the Id; sensual experience of the environment and the subsequent processing of it by the subjective mind via the Ego; and with intuitive acquisition of Being-sourced insights accessed through the Vig.

## The Id

Neurologist Sigmund Freud (1856-1939 CE), brought the subjective mind to the world's attention in his paper "Das Ich und das Es" ("The Ego and the Id"). The work served to provide a conceptual framework for contemporary psychoanalysis. For the purposes of AFT integration, however, the original notion of Freud's Id requires refinement and evolution from its original inception. In addition to Freud's initial notes and psychologist C.J. Jung's (1875-1961 CE) subsequent detailing of the animas (unconscious), I propose also that the Id is the vault of instincts and impulses that achieve momentum through the lineage-specific DNA imprinting unique to each person; these are the heritable protocols that are genetically encoded to offspring. According to AFT, DNA is the genetic repository for the entire bandwidth of residues from ancestral vibrations that directly influence our lives. In many ways (and for most individuals) this effect is typically experienced unconsciously. Indigenous cultures nearly all refer (and pray) to the "power of the ancestors" for intimate guidance, or for some intervening assistance from them when life becomes confusing or overwhelming. Before, and even after any notion of God or a mysterious "Great Spirit," tribal cultures leaned heavily on the *ancestors* for wisdom and benevolent insight. This genetic influence speaks to us through the somatic structure of the Id.

It is popular to perceive of conception as a "soulful" event, and that reincarnation explains past-life influences. However, the effect of past lives on an individual does not arise from a former personal life carried over as residual impressions on some transmigrational spirit. Impersonal awareness, or Being, carries no such residues from any incarnation, past or present, as Monad associations are ultimately dispersed after physical death. Though we are indeed influenced by past lives, the effect is purely biological. The cellular impact arises from ancestral vibrational influences sourced from our direct genetic lineage. There is also an indirect heritable influence from those who may have loved and deeply affected our ancestors, because love is a modifier to all master design elements. This is how consciousness affects DNA structures in evolutionary ways—which is why the alchemy of love is such a powerfully transformative aspect of human consciousness. These residues reverberate through generations by virtue of DNA vibrational saturations, and often reappear to enrich the lives of later generations of people.

Through purely impulse-driven prompting, the Id propels us without thought or inspiration into key instinctual action. Housed in the lower root chakra of the pelvic girdle, the AFT accounting of the Id has it giving rise to the base emotional content (strong aversion or compelling draw) of human expression. Human emotion has evolved over millennia to compose complex variations of the basic response of an organism to its environment—referring to them as *feelings*. Survival instinct and sexual drivers are the most deeply seated archetypes of Id functionality, and in more complex organisms like humans they retain a design capacity to be co-managed by higher seated chakra centers.

In AFT contexts, feeling is a subset of an organism's responsiveness to its environment, and the more complex the organism, the more sophisticated its responsive dimensionality. When we observe single cell organisms under a microscope, we see that they move and react to external stimuli in the surrounding environment.

They are (as we are) functioning from the most basic of protocols—repulsion and attraction. The innate responsiveness of "repel or draw" is the emotional foundation of the feelings we experience within the core of the human psyche. These archetypically responsive constituents are housed in the realm of the Id. Locating feeling and emotion is a fundamental aspect of unveiling the instinctual response that is alive within us. This is why emotional intelligence is so important toward finding clarity in human sentience.

**The Ego**

The Ego, another Freudian offspring, has become a commonplace term in English and American vernacular. When the word is used, it tends to refer to a personal sense of "I" asserting itself in a connotatively selfish or narcissistic way. There is no doubt that the Ego, left to its own devices, will typically fall into some degree of self-absorption. As I define it, the Ego consists of the conceptual constructs of the mind that lead to subjective paradigms (ideological projections). These concocted realities have a certain appeal to the operational functionality of the personality structures they inhabit. Subjective consciousness gathers together a coalition of abstractions and willfully orders them into a conceptual framework, which includes a personal platform to be utilized as a sense of self. But like an endless hall of mirrors, the Ego can get lost in its own fabrications. That distortion is almost guaranteed when the Ego is conducting itself without impersonal oversight. Like a rogue Lieutenant, the psyche runs around spouting orders outside the chain of command, dismissing the influence of Being and creating dissention and chaos within the ranks.

The Ego structure of human beings is a distinct creature. An individual's personal reality is often defined by a merry-go-round of memories and projections swirling around inside a closed system of compiled data and reaction programs. Gathered information is continually being measured against a base set of personal aversions and preferences that dictate reaction or response. Yet, an isolated conceptual paradigm is a restricted characteristic that inhibits an organically available quantum level of possibility to the human mind. Human sentience is simply not designed to be limited only to the operational parameters of the psyche. Yet, this narrow bandwidth of personality consciousness is where most human beings currently find themselves. This condition of partial awareness is affecting the population of the planet in very harmful ways.

The hallmark of the Ego as a coherent aspect of sentience is that it offers a sense of subjective functionality in time and space. Since it is the heart of the personal self, it is centrally seated in the body at the heart chakra. Subject-object relations emanate from this area because the heart represents the core aspect of physiological manifestation—and this hub governs subjective existence in time and space. In order to have relationship our hearts must be open to the systems we encounter. This is why the Ego, in AFT, is associated with the heart, and not with the head, as is typical from Freudian perspectives. It is the *whole* subjective presence that finds relationship with its environment, and the heart is the foundation of our entire dimensionality as created beings. A relatively recent error of our rational ancestors mistakenly assigned the ego to the mind. It is essential now that we reclaim our full sense of dimensional Presence by moving our sense of self out of the foster home of the head, and back into the natural home of the heart—the ego's organic center.

Without access to the natural integration of impersonal awareness fields, subjective fascination with thought consciousness becomes morbid, distorted and heavily fixated on conceptual paradigms. A human being that is functioning from this walled-off system of purely rational consciousness will feel "strangely off" to any creature that is in compliance with its own natural design. Depression, rage, psychic schisms and mental pathologies abound for human's who compartmentalize consciousness, and no one caught in this state can find relief, search as they may, from inside the system of thought. No amount of focus, will power, hypnosis, positive thinking, reprogramming, psychotropic drugs, mindful meditation, or cognitive therapy will ever affect a full healing or even a balanced expression of mental health functioning without finding depth consciousness through the compelling influence and artful integration of the pure awareness fields that abide prior to thought. The closed psychic system will normalize completely if, and when, individual consciousness becomes fully transparent to the impact and integration of the impersonal awareness of Being as accessed through the Vig.

## The Vig

The third correlative of human sentience is the intuitive factor of subjective awareness that AFT labels the *Vig*, from the Latin word *vigilare*—meaning a higher order of wakefulness. The Vig allows for an individually aligned consciousness to access the stillness of Being—a preeminent field of awareness that is transcendent of both the conceptual mind and the instinctive animus. The prime directive of the Vig is to offer a portal of transparency to nourishing Universal Intelligence. This feature is designed to be utilized as the sovereign seat of evolutionary consciousness in human beings. The physiological orientation is at the crown of the head because that location reflects the human body's prize capacity for abstract thought and self-reflection. It has become critically necessary for our species to consciously utilize the Vig as conductor to the gateway of Being, where it may sponsor our aptitude to remain consistently available to transcendent fields.

The sublime and impersonal realms of awareness accessed through the Vig have a tempering influence on the psyche. The Vig is the conduit for the still point of clear Presence that ultimately qualifies all action. Ralph Waldo Emerson alludes to our relationship with the Vig in his 1841 essay on the "Over-Soul." His 19th century treatment was most likely lost to his generation's relative inability to resonate with the subtle aspects of that writing's elegant elucidations. Though the understanding of Vig faculties still proves somewhat elusive to mainstream culture today, the age of Vig integration is now most certainly upon us.

Certain characteristics of the human brain are presenting a challenge to Vig utilization. The Vig, as a functional facet of sentience in our species becomes routinely hijacked by the neocortex and its random and dramatic capacity for abstract thinking. From pure awareness, the human mind creates conceptual paradigms utilizing the mechanism of its visualization attributes, generating either future projection, past recollection, or present fantasy. The typical human being is creating a virtual reality from thought (conceptual projections imposed on to real-time circumstances), out of sheer habit. Affirmed by linguistic systems that concretize patterns of belief, likes, and dislikes, we pathologically assert ourselves through these language-enhanced ideological constructs. Without the essential governor of Vig oversight discerning our perceptions and conduct in the world, the false pretense of this ordered distortion becomes the fulcrum of our experience. The Vig is the appropriate seat of clarity through which we may select for coherent frequency in thought and action. It is essential that we dispense with the false Ego-based protocol that selects for thought solely based on its propensity for the acquisition of pleasure—combined with an aversion to almost everything else. Until then, the renegade personality structure will continue to color the subjective sense of "I" outside the lines meant to contain coherent expression.

It is important here to note that this mythological sense of one's identity cannot locate itself without the mind indulging projections in time. Time itself has become the signature sting of "I." A fabricated sense of existence propels itself through time sponsored by internal motivators that avoid pain while pursuing comfort and familiar routine. These archetypal psychic patterns are energized by the Id's prime directive: The genetically hardwired instincts for survival and propagation. This drive presses the subjective sense of self into a complex collusion of ideas that takes no notice of anything outside the graphic interface of the senses and subsequent emotional/intellectual processing toward achieving those primal urges. This is the much-touted "fall from grace," where the subtler and more expansive aspects of Being accessed through the Vig have either been forgotten, or never cultivated in the first place. As such, we have become hypnotized by the colorful drama of the personal self careening through life. In such conditions the fragmentation from Source awareness creates anxieties in the psyche that express as emotionally charged perceptions of powerlessness, overwhelm, loneliness, despair, rage, melancholy, helplessness, confusion, exhaustion, hopelessness and apathy.

There can be no realization of peace when individuals experience themselves solely through a sense of the limited psychic platform that is disconnected from the deeper dimension of Source awareness. When we are relating to life as an imagined self, mired in stories and processing existence through the time-related themes of projection and reflection, we are not actualizing full consciousness. In such limited states we can never know ourselves to be any deeper than the narrative of self that we have created in our conceptual mind's eye. We must utilize the Vig to effect integration of psychic structures, and to govern the personal instrument through phenomena. From an AFT perspective, Vig regulation of the subjective self is the "holy grail" of human evolution.

Vig guidance consists of the vigilant review of the Ego's psychic produce by impersonal awareness fields. The craft involves an ongoing and continual culling of the full harvest of moment-to-moment thoughts and feelings, to locate those conceptual movements that contain vibrational rapport with stillness (Being). Through this process we learn to energize and actualize those thoughts and feelings that are harmonic to the field of Creative Intelligence we touch into through Being. Vig sovereignty over subjective machinations is a design characteristic our species must eventually evolve. The time is now ripe for a large portion of the population to discover our organic orientation to the subtlety of Being through Vig interface. Yet when moving through this terrain we must be careful to avoid *preferential states*.

It must be understood that the sentient systems of the Vig, Ego, and Id are complementary systems. There is a tendency for the faculties of high reason and logic to want to place these operational centers into some kind of hierarchy. It is a debilitating miscalculation to make. We must not confuse the essential nature of the Vig's role as a complementary system to other sentient properties by seeing it as the only legitimate system to emphasize. Such practice results in the unhealthy negation, or attempted domination over the other two aspects of sentience that operate from the Id and Ego. The trifecta must be allowed to be radically open and available to one another, and not undergo selective prioritization in significance—one over another. Mutual influence of these systems is critical for the design algorithms of human sentience to organically actualize. So even though I sometimes refer to Vig integration as "sovereign" in this chapter due to its critical contribution to the coherent expression of consciousness, the essential factor is meaningless without the subjective correlative of unmitigated Id and Ego participation. In short, we must be careful not to slip into the "spiritual" trap of preferring Vig sublimations. The operational systems of sentience are a whole movement in harmony, not a model of hierarchy in action.

In summation, we see that organisms are informed at three levels of being. The Id operates at the level of DNA, where genetic encoding activates cellular and instinctual functionality. The Ego functions through the psychological level of empirical learning where experiences gathered through the senses remind the subjective self of how to perform in the environment with less pain and increased efficiency. The third and least integrated aspect of sentience in humans comes from the pure field of Creator-Intelligence-Presence that informs the crucible of our individual consciousness—where the Vig accesses Being. ✸

# CHAPTER 10
# Being

*B*eing, the sublime extension of Noumenal Awareness is referred to liberally throughout The 5th Phenomenon. Being, as seen through the lens of AFT, is an impersonal field of awareness that exists preeminently to individual consciousness. Being is associated with all life and is synonymous with the QFP matrix, just as Monad is associated with all life and is synonymous with TPC. In our species, Being is accessed in the body through the Vig. Deriving one's sense of consciousness from Being means that the instrument of the human body and all its respective sentient faculties must be attenuated to the stillness of Being. Integrating Being, contrary to much spiritual dogma, does not annihilate Ego—it simply preempts it. Being abides as the organic default nature of human consciousness. Being, as we have defined it, is different from the Monad, or what so many have referred to as soul or the spirit of a person. A Monad by contrast is the personal awareness component that affixes to an organism at conception, and falls away when the organism dies. Being is the ubiquitous and impersonal matrix of Presence that animates QFP.

Being is wedded intimately to the Intelligence of the Creator, and as such moves harmoniously within the sublime algorithms of creation. It does not, however, participate in the aversion or attraction residues of subjective sentience. An individual's consciousness may move back and forth from clarity of Being to the delusions and distortions of the isolated psyche routinely. This means that one is either in clarity or in varying degrees of distortion within that pattern of oscillation. Though Being is absolute pristine awareness, when tapped by the unconscious actor through a personality structure that is not integrated, Being's profound potential for clear expression becomes sadly reduced to the plodding task of *animating* the distortions of divergent psychic structures.

It is important to note that Being does not insist that human sentience emphasize expression of its own design capacity for conscious clarity. Impersonal Awareness harbors no ploy to direct subjective consciousness to become self-realized or to establish the "enlightenment" of the organism it animates. The unfolding of human sentience is an equation that defies the notions of "free will" *and* that of "divinely ordained fate." The *free will versus fate* squabble is merely the personality structure's attempt to argue with itself by generating more mind-based distractions to stay outside the direct experience of depth consciousness. A holistic integration of Being requires no such rationalizations, and when we are in total communion with that Presence we become liberated from the need for postured intellectual discrimination.

Until we realize release into clarity, the control machinations of the subjective persona assert themselves with an array of fabricated stories that they cling to. These intrigues become the birthplace of belief—and by extension ideological violence. When one individual's belief aligns with another's, we see the formation of allies. Where one person's beliefs contradict or otherwise oppose another's, enemies arise. Being has no interest in any of this, and if we are to evolve, we must eventually plunge into the heart of impersonal awareness fields that free our consciousness from becoming captured by the isolated operations of the personal mind that compulsively conceives ideas in opposition.

To that end, the most important aspect of learning the art of integrating whole sentience is discovering the kinesthetic feel of impersonal awareness. This sense of Being orders on the sublime, so it is helpful to discover some somatic cues. In my own experience, attenuating to Being means to search internally for a non-specific vibrational tone, a kind of harmonic frequency that is akin to the relaxation one feels upon awaking out of a deep sleep. There is the feel of physical, albeit subtle, oscillations of serenity. It expresses as a non-localized quality of palpable tranquility, a product of the coherent alignment of localized personal consciousness with the nourishing background of pristine Noumenal Awareness.

Scanning the bandwidth of the thinking mind we can likewise discover thoughts with a similar tonal concordance to stillness, and we may select for them instead of other thoughts that do not appear to be in such vibrational accord. Conducting life in this way, by flowing with the Tao of harmonic thought and feeling selections, (by listening *from* Being, and not *to* Being,) we embody the art of living that leads to an aligned and fluid expression. As harmonic consciousness waxes, there is no longer such a compelling draw to our idea of things. The wandering mind no longer commands the kind of attention that used to elicit reaction without spacious deliberation. We become mature, in the deepest sense of the word, and available to the Creative Presence to graduate us into deeper consciousness and clarity. We are approaching a readiness to be subsumed by Being. Watch a log burn in the fireplace, and you will witness the subsuming of matter to energy. Similarly, the sublimation of our thought-driven, hyper-existence consciousness to the sovereignty of Being is a consuming process that induces a transformative stillness at the very seat of the experiencer.

There is no detailed accounting for the process of being subsumed by pure awareness. One cannot know for certain when or how the algorithm will unfold. One must be patient, for the delivery of such freedom cannot be realized by willing it into fruition. Subsumed by Being does not mean we simply determine to move or live beyond our bodies. The keynote of this process is contingent upon the depth of surrender. The formula is unalterable. The quality of surrender at this level is no longer about the ego's concept of surrender any more than a peach can be harvest-ready by merely thinking about ripeness (if a peach could think). What makes one human evolve is ever a mystery. The equations are deliberately non-specific, and the epic algorithms will never be fully understood within such orders. It is both appropriate and beautiful that the persistent thrust of consciousness through living matter is one of the most mystical aspects of creation.

When I was a child of 4 or 5 years old, I was swept out to sea by a large wave while building sandcastles at the surf's edge. The wave grabbed me like a hungry monster and pulled me into the rolling ferocity of its huge, watery belly. I remember suddenly tumbling inside a turbulent world of blue and green churning, but I was not afraid. I did not experience fear because I had not the slightest idea of what was happening to me. I was so preoccupied with my sandcastles that I never saw the wave coming. Inside the rolling mass of seawater, with eyes wide open, I continued to breathe. During the whole episode I was watching with wonder the tumultuous aqua-blue spectacle all around me. I was eventually rescued, and the water expelled from my lungs on the beach, but I cite this instance because when one is subsumed by Being it is a bit like that experience. In such moments, one has no sense of fear regarding surviving the ordeal, or even being separate from it as a *thing* in opposition. One takes in the whole experience as it is unfolding without story, because there is no impulse to hold to the known and the familiar. Having directly experienced such exquisite sublimations, one must then be careful not to covet them as a desirable state.

Genuine integration of Being is often threatened, ironically, by the perennial seductions of concept spirituality—that which would seek attainment by capturing some position of assumed realization. Many spiritual seekers are quick to self-assess a sense of self-mastery and feel as though they have arrived to some place of completion when they first touch into Being consciously. Some of these individuals even go on to become pundits, write books, or garner reputations as trend-worthy personalities. Yet there is often a nuanced deception in such instances. One might infer a covert failure on the part of the proclaimed figure to continue moving deeper into the experience of life, because there has been a stalling at the witnessing state. This is why many self-declared "consciousness teachers" feel to me as if they have no edge, displaying a postured pretense that suggests that they are seamlessly unaffected by this life because they claim to move only from the impersonal. This is not what occurs when one is genuinely subsumed by Being. True sublimation opens to a uniform functionality of all awareness field systems in harmony, from the subjective to the impersonal. We must not dabble in impersonal awareness fields just to escape feeling life, or to seek some reputation of cultured aloofness from it. Subsumed by Being means that all dimensions of human sentience are fully open and engaged, and not fixated on one distinct field, adulating it as predominantly superior to other aspects of consciousness.

We must be ruthlessly honest in our reach for authentic clarity. If we were to take inspiration from the legendary Christ, we do not simply arrive at some elevated state of consciousness and hang out with like-minded followers in comfortable surroundings, affirming each other's enlightened intentions with feather soft tonal exchanges. We instead engage in the perfect storm of *depth consciousness*. We speak with a fire that is particular to the fuel of the moment, and not in those familiar platitudes of the spiritual subculture. Real integrity might even mean that we move provocatively in the face of convention and social authority, not submitting to the rendering of obvious answers to garner safety, praise or solidarity. To move genuinely from Being is to feel our actual emotions, even if that means we must sweat blood in the garden, or suffer the deep betrayals of our heart-given trust. Radically following our truth might lead us to flip the tables of corruption, while simultaneously accepting the true fate that is assigned to us. This art prompts us to feel the depth of our personal preferences, but to do so in the light of an impersonal awareness that is simultaneously conveying deep wisdom. We may very well find some dirt under our nails and blood at our feet along the way. Yet it is not necessary to withdraw from the force of our psychic systems to the perceived sanctuary of impersonal awareness to take refuge from the total experience of our existence. We need not hide from life behind the subtle aspects of our being. ✪

# CHAPTER 11
# God

Our life is a one-way journey of aging, culminating in death. The stark snapshot of our existence prompts us to seek some meaning inherent in the confluence of moments that comprise our life—some reconciling perhaps of the sum of its parts. Enter the notion of God, heaven and the afterlife. But just what is this meaning so feverishly sought after through the ideas of God? I would suggest that people grasping at images of the divine in order to discover some existential reckoning have not yet moved away from the exiguous drone of their unexamined lives and collapsed with abandon into the heart of their own existence.

The age-old question of God only arose when our species dreamed up notions of divinity from some imaginary point of reference they took to be themselves. Before the awkward sense of "I" ever existed, there was no divine dilemma to argue about, or over. The whole proposition that there is a god to deny or prove has been the conspired fabrication of both believers and atheists alike. In fact, the core existential quandary has never been about concepts of god. The pathology arises because of the inception and propagation of the *idea* of a separate self that seemingly struggles with its own existence. A human being functioning out of genuine clarity neither requires nor desires the idea of God, because that individual directly experiences the Creative Presence moment to moment—a state which invokes the serenity that dispels all angst. No one needs to believe in a sun when they are feeling the warmth of the sunshine on their skin.

It is true that Creator Presence is sublime by nature, and not capable of being fully apprehended by the mind of man, but the personality structure too quickly dismisses the dimensional aspect. This places an individual in a predicament of incompleteness, where the psyche feels compelled to "find itself," all while yoked with the twin task of simultaneously trying to find a god to receive salvation from. These become the lifelong shadows that we chase—apparitions that exist nowhere but in the incessant projections of the thinking mind. And so the question persists, how do we reconcile or locate the living source of creative Intelligence that is behind this awe-inspiring spectacle if typical rumination about God is merely a depiction of our imagination? How can we learn to enjoy a direct experience with the Creator without having some idea of that relationship getting in the way?

The purest teaching uses wisdom to liberate the learner from all ideas. The seduction of conceptual absolutes ever dams the mighty current of clarity available to all of us. Isolated thinking has become a barrier that brings the free-flowing torrent of living Presence to a murky standstill inside our consciousness. This suffocating inertia confounds our natural capacity to fluidly engage a proper relationship with the essence of Creator Presence. Thought immersion and obsession is causing us to forfeit vital intimacy with the Being-nurtured beauty, grace, and wisdom that is the organic endowment of human beings. We are as eagles, living like pigs in a muddy corral. Our core instinct senses the divine updrafts, only to find that our wings have become cumbersome and useless at our sides. We toggle around in the soil of thought moment to moment, layering our delicate feathers of flight in heavy conceptual earth. It is this morass of thinking in which we bury ourselves routinely that makes the real availability of flight just a fairytale. Yet, Creator Presence is no myth. The sublime fields of pristine awareness are alive and waiting for us to shake off all the dusty ground of the mind so that we may finally sense into the soaring potential of conscious expression that is our birthright as human beings. And we must *sense* this, because we will always be closer to a genuine existence by *feeling* Creator Presence than we will ever be to *thinking* the idea of God into our lives.

Contemplations about God have historically been perceived as the highest form of intellectual enterprise. Philosophers continue to approach notions of God in cleverly complicated ways. High-minded dialectics on divinity tend to involve those who align themselves with the philosophy du jour. Materialist spars with idealist, who spars with dualist, who spars with non-dualist, who spars with the proponent of panpsychism. Christian theologians argue to this day over the ideologically contrived *divine nature* of Jesus. Yet there is no record of Jesus ever deliberating on the "hypostatic union of the holy trinity" which many secular scholars vehemently declare he must have embodied. With regard to all of the intellectual jousting, are we really any closer to intimacy with the living Spirit of God that Jesus *did* speak of?

Where in fact, is the life in all this philosophic and religious rhetoric? Observe the quality of energy emerging from those engaged in the typically aggressive discourse around these subjects; discern if they feel cumbersome and unnatural to the senses. Ecclesiastical treatments addressing the divine seem to me as if a computer took it upon itself to describe making love—it all sounds good, but one gets the distinct feeling that the source agent hasn't really been there. Does talking academically *about* a god really establish a direct experience *with* God? Does a purely intellectual approach to the subject of divinity ever work to establish a place inside the speaker from where one can speak with true authority about relationship with the mystical aspects of existence? The purely rational examination inevitably lacks intimacy, and where there is no intimacy there can be no relationship that establishes rapport with all dimensions of our consciousness.

The saying goes that to really love another (to have a truly intimate relationship with them) you have to be able to love yourself. This is also true when engaging a relationship with the Creator. But what exactly does it mean to love one's self? AFT would suggest it is an intimate association with the full dimensionality of one's complete consciousness. To appreciate our existence in this way is to experience one's self as deeper than the components of personality. One must be intimate with every aspect of one's existence, including those beyond the physical properties of the body and corresponding psyche. AFT asserts that there is a dimension of transpersonal awareness from which the very foundation of our sentience is derived—divinely described or not. We must be aware, open, and intimately available to these realms of our existence. Then we will be prepared for a conscious and direct experience with the Presence so much of the world calls "God," because it is in this fashion of communion where all ideas of God become useless.

This is why the Tao (with regard to the *Tao Te Ching*) approaches an art of self-understanding without deity conceptualization. The Tao points instead to a wonder and reverence for creation, through intimate observation of the balance and order of all phenomenal systems. The Tao invites us to consider a direct experience of Life without the need for an interpretive agency to explain it to us. What need a rabbi tell us about the colors of a sunset? What beauty can a priest impart to us about the smell of a rose that we could not, or should not, fathom on our own?

There is no goal within the Tao, as there is no object of worship. The 8th century exegesis *Tao T'i Lun* not withstanding, the first teachings of the Tao rank as one of the most motive-free philosophical approaches to clarity. And yet, for all its reveries, even the *Tao Te Ching* at moments lifts its finger off the pulse of wise actualization in the world. Chuang-Tze (also known as Zhuangzi) counsels us through the concept of *Wu-wei*, that the sage does not occupy himself with worldly affairs. Though the emphasis is on the clear reception by the experiencer of the nuanced order of creation, the philosophy comes up short with regard to speaking into the requisite art of subjectively integrating those musings into the body for practical use in social life.

In any case, the bulk of humanity does not find existential consolation in the expressions of the elegant, though god-less philosophy of the Tao, preferring instead the prolific precepts of theistic doctrines to grasp onto and believe in. Until we can achieve a compelling direct experience of the Creator for ourselves, the mind will be drawn to an indirect experience of the "concept" of a god as proxy for true intimacy with our Source. But the mandate is clear; in the end, we must all return to the Creator, while embodied, as children of that Intelligence—and that movement must be *responsive*, not willful. Through this form of receptivity we will come to know that our natural relationship with Life is very intimate, even as it is sublimely impersonal. Reconciling the longing/aversion pathology the subjective self has toward the ambiguous aspects of Being is incredibly significant to our sentient evolution. At some point in our journey we must all face the powerfully personal choice about whether the singular becomes subsumed by the whole at the final threshold of our personal consciousness. Some will shrink away from even the possibility of such a radical transmutation. Others long for this subtle release so profoundly that they may go to whatever extremes they can find in an attempt to leverage even some semblance of its actualization.

Today in Antarctica there are around thirty countries manning seventy or so multinational bases that conduct benevolent scientific research. With the exception of isolated patches of Antarctic hair grass and pearlwort, the continent could easily be characterized as a frozen desert. Home to brutal winds that result in a desiccated landscape, the southern ice cap holds ninety percent of the world's ice. The summertime research population of the frozen continent averages a mere four thousand people, and the winter season reduces that number to about a thousand intrepid souls who hunker down for a long, dark winter. During the cold season the continent doubles in size with accumulated ice, and there is simply no way in or out of Antarctica for over six months. In late March the sun sinks and does not break the nighttime horizon again to dawn a new day until September. Those who choose to remain in this hostile environment during the Antarctic winter are an interesting breed. With no direct sunlight for approximately 170 days, they forgo the natural circadian rhythms that we as humans evolved under. There is a sense that the individuals who make up these stalwart adventurers eschew the frenetic affairs of civilization. In spite of the brutally harsh conditions and minimalist lifestyle, they choose to remain in this freezing cold, dim, and relatively lifeless place, volunteering to be stranded there in self-imposed exile for months. What is in it for them?

The common sentiment among these sojourners is that in this isolated world there is a compelling stillness and stark beauty available to them. Perhaps that exquisite sense is born of the psychological restraint brought about by the extreme environmental conditions that exist there. Antarctica offers the visitor a primordial solitude; a guileless splendor that would likely be directly compromised by the comforts that are readily available on the other commodity-abundant continents of the world. On Antarctica they forgo leisure, control, and cultural nourishment for the strident tranquility that encompasses them in those coveted months. The ascetic sabbatical becomes an austere journey into a peace that typically eludes them in normal society. It is beautiful, and ironic to see humans adapt to such severe landscapes to find the tender aspects of our existence. Those dauntless souls in Antarctica demonstrate how committed we can be to finding mystically contented repose, even at great danger or cost. Inside the lucid silence, they are reaching for the thread that brings us home to true Presence. More than religion, deeper than philosophy, the human spirit longs for pure communion with the Creator.

Our individual consciousness is like a seed. There is a dormant potential inside each of us, just waiting for the right conditions to burst forth and reach up into life, while at the same time driving taproots deeper into the ground from which we emerge. There is an innate responsiveness in everyone waiting to bloom and live in accord with our complete organic design. And so the seeds of our abundance quietly lay in the dark and soil-less drawers of our intellect, anticipating the springtime of our evolution when they will be sown into the fertile soil of Presence and grow. And grow they will. So tall that eventually they will reach up and touch the face of creation without thought—without volition. This heaven-on-earth is immediate, and as Jesus said, "It is at hand." Waiting for a physical death for the gift of life to be bestowed in some conjured afterlife with God is more than absurd, it is a missed opportunity.

With AFT, we may ponder an existence that does not need to *contemplate* God because it is in direct and living communion with that Intelligence moment to moment. This unfolds a world where we do not require temples or mosques or churches to commune with the Spirit of creation that lives through and around everything. The sacred no longer becomes provincial or proprietary, because there is no place for such partition in the eternal mind. With this evolution, we begin to finally reflect a conscious harmony with our Source. What if we all knew God as simply "The Is That Does." There is a refreshing guilelessness in the statement that is hard to build a church around—and it suggests an intimacy with the Creator that requires no sophistications of thought or device to manifest. In such a space, we become the sole agent of our own distinct dance with the divine. Here, there is nothing to fight over, because nothing can be taken away. ✪

# Chapter 12
# Existential Schisms & Mental Health

A human being's foremost folly is the belief that their imagined sense of self exists as a sole and primary reality. It is the mind's assertion of this personal concept that creates the tension from which fear and anxiety are born. The psyche persists in trying to define reality on its own terms because the fluid field of impersonal awareness abiding prior to embodiment is far too sublime for Ego-based perception to ever reconcile. Conversely, the subjective self does not possess the capacity to confine and limit pure awareness attributes inside conceptual machinations. This is why the mind continues to indulge its propensity to become lord of its own projected world, at the cost of shunning Creator Presence. Through AFT we may confirm and discover the craft of relaxing into the spaciousness of awareness fields around the mind, allowing us finally to escape the prisons of our own making.

To truly realize freedom outside of psychic distortions is to directly experience the clarity of living Presence that is at the heart of our sentience—that awareness which is prior to thought. The operational Intelligence inherent in pure awareness is of an entirely different order than the brain's limited and temporally-bound system of thought. Being a "smart" individual is the pale and distant relative of Creator Intelligence. To ground our specific consciousness in impersonal awareness is to be directly enlightened by the living Presence behind the design of the universe itself. To be severed from that nourishing field is to wither our fertile mind and relegate our existence to a life of rational banality.

Indeed, human beings that live solely out of a psychic reality, act out of an ascertainable complexion that is so superficial, much of their patterned relating can be mapped if one pays attention to it. That is because a mind disjoined from Presence is a relatively static and predictable system. For anyone who finds that they are conducting this version of scripted life, the most compelling activity available to them would be discovering the spontaneity of a radical aliveness derived from the influence of Presence. According to AFT, that movement turns out to be more of an art than a science—more of an ongoing fluid discernment than an act of singular achievement.

It is an incredible occurrence for a radically free awareness to be affixed to a self-reflexive mind that is bound in time and space. The reconciling of this dichotomy is what our evolutionary potential is calling for. Until we actualize the artful integration of AFT, we will continue to endure the hellish fragmentation of psychosis that is the mind's idea of itself acting as a separate thing. Through the nature of such splintered consciousness we become lost in ourselves, grinding a cold reality out of an erroneous conceptual framework. The tension that is created by virtue of this fundamental error will continue to birth the existential schisms that drive all our woes.

Much of what is today described as mental illness has its roots in this form of schism. We operate out of conceptual paradigms while simultaneously walling off conscious integration with the larger fluid field of impersonal awareness we are immersed in. This unnatural distancing from Presence eventually leads to pathological dynamics within the personality, expressing as dissociative psychic structures that become fixated and habitual. What is actually occurring is the routine self-imposed isolation of thought from the full dimensional capacity of human consciousness. The act is facilitating an inorganic fragmentation of sentience that inevitably produces violence. Such schisms are born of the hyper-utilization of frontal lobe visualization capacities *without* Vig oversight. The intense mental activity of projections without the objective review of impersonal awareness can trigger the descent of the subjective persona into various distortions of mental illness. These diseases progress when routine awareness is used to energize the compartmentalization of these psychotic landscapes, causing them to be perceived and confirmed by the personality structure as separate and apart from the field of general Presence. That distortion can deepen critically over time until Being itself becomes dismissed or forgotten by the psyche altogether. The dynamic defining this schism is degrading human sentience, and has been for millennia.

General psychosis will abscond with the animating facets of Presence by partitioning subset abstractions of the thinking mind before legitimizing them as a perceived reality. Though these fabrications are entirely incoherent, the mind packages them into an ordered conceptual paradigm to live out of. This dynamic is rendering partially integrated psyches that are moving outside of whole consciousness. Whenever these distortions produce patterned behavior that is socially acceptable, the individual is seen to be conforming to convention, and their actions are deemed normative— even though the behaviors are *conceived* in violence. If the schism sourced behavior disrupts trending social zeitgeist for any reason, then such expression is diagnosed as problematic and converted to a pathology in the DSM-V. Whether behaviors are deemed "normal" or "pathological," the actions are still derived from schisms within human sentience. In these instances it is the quality of general consciousness that needs to be addressed—diagnosing dysfunctional behavior patterns for treatment is crisis management, it is not problem solving.

Whenever a personality structure chooses to isolate and descend into the hypnotic drama of conceptual machinations, it will always forgo the radical clarity that brings coherent expression. Psychic disassociation from full dimension consciousness is a hallmark of every mental and emotional health condition where the brain is not injured or impaired. At the core of such psychosis is a control-oriented struggle where the Ego is desperately trying to stave off the interfacing of personal psychic structures with the expanded fields of awareness.

In addressing mental illness through an AFT perspective, we must be clear that thought and visualization attributes are not problematic by design. Indeed, conceptualization is a primary aspect of human evolution, and one that has allowed our species to dominate all others on the planet. But when this mechanism for projecting abstractions begins to manufacture a subset of reality that believes its own myth of separation from Source, the schism that defines general psychotic pathology is born. Healthy expression is compromised under such conditions and even in cases where profound insight is bestowed upon an individual suffering from such detached consciousness, there manifests a debilitating effect of the transmission value. The compromise arises due to the incomplete consciousness that is sponsoring or receiving the inspired content.

Modern psychology has stepped in to label and define the varied patterns of psychic distortion that result from schisms within the human awareness field system without understanding the premise of Awareness Field Theory. There is tremendous value in detailing patterns of mental and emotional disharmony, to be sure. Yet, the mental health profession will need to move beyond the labeling of pathologies and its subsequent fixation with inorganic remedies (pharmaceuticals) if it is to make any real headway toward restoring true health and balance to those suffering from these conditions. Awareness Field Theory offers a deeper contribution toward the coherency of psychological expression than do all the current medicines and cognitive and somatic therapies combined. That is because AFT engages the core issue—*fragmented consciousness*. Therapists in this field should first apply to their own lives the fundamental practice of living directly out of the clarity of Being as presented in *The 5th Phenomenon*, and then begin integrating those dimensional understandings into the niche studies of psychotherapy and psychology. When that era arrives, the mental health profession will finally graduate into an industry of genuine service. The contemporary field of depth psychology will in time be subsumed by the broader, more penetrating study of *depth consciousness* work detailed in AFT.

It is unfortunate to consider how tired traditional psychotherapy has become in the last forty years. The counseling profession today has simply stalled. It stands relatively helpless in the face of a pandemic of a global psycho-emotional disharmony it cannot begin to manage. There is a mass existential crisis that feels as if it is approaching apocalyptic proportion—billions of humans are clamoring for coping strategies. Pharmaceutical abuse has now become so pervasive that teenagers have learned how to diagnose themselves with online research so that they know exactly what to say to their parents, physicians and therapists to get desired drugs they read about on the Internet or hear about from friends. The case for PhD-level mental health psychiatry and psychology fares no better. I suspect that these industry practitioners mean well in spirit, but without the necessary dimensional enrichment of Awareness Field Theory, they will continue lumbering along with the barren protocols of psychological stabilization techniques, setting the low bar of therapeutic goals to the obtuse determinations of "normative" functioning.

The study of consciousness I reveal in *The 5th Phenomenon* has never endeavored to achieve a state of psychologically defined "normalcy" for an individual. Nor has it pursued the typically sought after functional "stabilization" that the Diagnostic and Statistical Manual of Mental Disorders (DSM-V) would set as a standard for "progress" or healing. Yet results from people exposed to the approaches expounded in AFT continually astonish me. The evolutions out of emotional and psychological disharmony they demonstrate are often so immediate and profound that I can sincerely say that I remain uncertain as to any limitation with regard to the healing capacity of AFT consciousness work. The key difference with AFT is that we are recognizing the relationship between the mind and the field of awareness that animates it, while psychology remains entirely confined and limited to cognitive approaches from inside the box of thought.

There is an amusing story from my childhood I sometimes share. My brother-in-law (a generation older than myself) was at one time a large machinery diesel mechanic. He worked on these colossal tractors with wheels that were easily twice as tall as a grown man. I remember when I was a kid and he turned to me one day while working on one of these huge machines and said with all due irony, "Always be bigger than what you are working on." No truer words were ever spoken. When the psyche *is* the problem, we had better find a larger reference point to engage the issue. Trying to cure subjective mental disorder with objective mental analysis (curing thought with thought) is like trying to clean a polluted river with a fishing net; you may scoop out a portion of the detritus, but in the end the river is still fundamentally toxic, and you have not solved the core problem. We must move beyond remedies derived by naked reason, be they concocted pharmaceutical remedies, or our own fascination with the mind's notion that it can fix itself. Controlling thought, or having a counselor/therapist attempt to help manage psycho-emotional states, is not true healing or recovery; it is at best the temporary pseudo-stabilization of a precarious psychic functionality. As long as the fundamental *dis-ease* of fragmented consciousness remains unaddressed (psychic structures not integrated with Presence), complete mental health simply cannot be achieved. Sadly, today most all personality structures remain severed from the vital harmonizing influence of impersonal awareness to some degree, and it is gravely affecting our evolution.

There is no doubt that the bulk of human relations currently consists of the frenetic cross projections of assumed ideas, fabricated identities, and latent and not-so-latent aversions and desires. All of these disconnected conceptual and impulsive mechanisms are rooted in an existential angst arising from a false sense of separation from the complete field of awareness that represents the full extent of our true nature. Poet and philosopher Henry David Thoreau (1817-1862 CE) called this peculiar order of anxiety the life of "quiet desperation" that most of us lead. That desperation comes from the fundamental disconnect of our personally derived identities from the core depth of consciousness that is naturally composed of Creative Intelligence. When we predicate the entire reality of our existence on something as incomplete as isolated ideas, and react to one another in association with the impulses surrounding those projections, we are all bound to suffer.

Human beings want so much to believe that their imagined tales of life are real; they want their assumptions to be absolute truth. Broken psyches are often so wedded to their notions of things that even in the face of irrefutable evidence contradicting their illusions, they will still choose to let themselves be duped, cajoled, fooled or otherwise lied to by anyone or anything that might serve to maintain the fantasy they have invested so heavily in. Over and over, people kneel at the altar of propaganda in supplication to anyone from politicians to psychics, just to affirm their desired point of view. As dire as the consequences can be for this critical self-deception, again and again human beings are willing to pay the price for this carnival sleight of hand.

Breaking out of such a servile existence and striking deeper into full Presence requires the cultivated capacity to let go of our mental fixations, and drop down into the core of our existence where the absolute essence of Being moves. AFT suggests we do this by following the thread of our own Creator-endowed system of awareness. This field of sentience extends straight through our personal subjective conceptual constructs, deeper than our unconscious memories and future projections, transcending even the basic instincts of survival impulses. Ultimately, this light of consciousness finds its way like a salmon, back to its source. But unlike salmon, our true Source is not the spawning ground of physical birth, but instead the non-locatable Presence that is the genesis of the Universe itself, from where all things have arisen. To be fully connected to this aspect of Being means to have seen through and integrated all the temporal realities that both horrify and enchant the mortal self. Such has been the suggested accomplishment of the Christ and Buddha personas that have, according to legend, succeeded in mastering this art of awareness while in a physical body. In spite of the myths surrounding these figures, I do not perceive such endeavors to be religious or even spiritual acts, but rather a movement arising out of a profoundly authentic personal mandate to deeply connect to the fundamentally true nature of existence itself.

The primary obstacle to cultivating the art of living in full consciousness is the imposed digression of thought without Presence. This issue, compounded by the mind's propensity (and inability) to achieve liberation from itself, produces an inescapable imbroglio. This quandary alone ought to give us sufficient pause to redirect our attention to seek solutions to mental schisms somewhere beyond the intellect. The secondary challenge is the conceptual self's inability to reconcile the collection of unknowns that inherently arise when confronted with the groundless nature of Being. This psychic aversion to subtle dimensions creates an ongoing tension in the mind, and if indulged too far, will begin a debilitating descent into the abyss of a precarious unconsciousness that is in conflict with its own nature. This distortion can also exacerbate dissociative character disorders when one becomes caught in the struggle to suppress and control the crescendo of ever-heightening and irreconcilable anxiety. Yet the imperative remains: *Personal consciousness can never become enlightened.* But from the point of view of the Ego, a fully sublimated subjective consciousness will always be a fate worse than death. For the isolated psyche, integration of the impersonal field of awareness is the end of the magnificent charade—an abomination that seems to impose upon the separate sense of self a personal powerlessness combined with conscious annihilation. To be certain, thought consciousness will "not go gentle into that good night," to quote poet Dylan Thomas (1914-1953 CE).

In John Sarno's (1923-2017 CE) book *The Divided Mind*, the physician, professor and author speaks about the relationship between the resistant and compartmentalizing Ego structure and the overall health of the body, with the mind's "…tendency to repress, rather than feel painful emotion… emotions we keep from our awareness… without conscious perception or outlet, [they] persist with us for a lifetime." Sarno, in this instance, is referring to the root cause of hypertension. He points out that stressful days, or even prolonged stressful events, may not be the real cause of disease (as in "stress kills"), but rather the real problem lies in the mind's concerted tactics not to feel the full scope of content surging within the emotional body. The Ego-structure, through a thought-driven willfulness, often attempts to resist feeling certain states through routine psychic dismissal, culminating in a repression that sentences the emotions to solitary confinement inside the dark cellars of the unconscious—where real *disease* begins. The psyche's dismissal of impersonal awareness fields occurs in similar fashion, manifesting as a rejection of the ineffable but nourishing dimensions of consciousness.

Just to be acutely aware of these kinds of distortions however, can be a huge step toward clarity. The light of clear, free consciousness when directed at any condition of the body is extremely healing. What is more, it also catalyzes permanent evolution.

In the long view, neither I, nor the work of AFT are primarily concerned with confronting or displacing the Ego, but moreover to deliver human sentience into the full dimensional depths of awareness—by bathing individual consciousness in the ubiquitous Presence of the Creator. I have come to acknowledge and honor that every person is a mysterious calculation, with uniqueness appropriate to each individual; an unfolding that might be compared to the same algorithm that governs the ways in which weather materializes. There is a general protocol of process where all variables matter; but at the same time nothing is the absolute determiner. For us humans, the virtues of *patience, humility, integrity* and *commitment* are certainly powerful personal ingredients we can cultivate to influence the equation. Perhaps this is why so many religious, spiritual and philosophical bodies of work tout those qualities. ✪

# CHAPTER 13
# Philosophy, Consciousness, Spirituality & Self Help

**Philosophy**

I find it telling that some of the purest existential introspections arise out of very distant times. The ancient Indian Vedas (originating approximately in the 12th century BCE) and various Gitas contain a plethora of metaphorically profound instruction ranging from the esoterically subtle and deeply mystical, to the ploddingly pragmatic. The Tao Te Ching (approximately the 2nd century BCE) is one of my favorite treatments of pure receptivity to existence. I also delight in the ruminations of the Greek contemplative Pyrrho (360-270 BCE), perhaps one of the most underrated philosophers in history. Many modern academics reduce Pyrrho's teachings to a convenient and cumbersome review known as *Pyrrhonian Skepticism*. But Pyrrho's hard earned wisdom could hardly be construed as a mere attitude of mind. I see Pyrrho as espousing a conscious receptivity to whatever presents itself in such a way that subjective clarity never assumes a posture of absolutism. His insight is clean, coherent and amazingly on point for his day. His notion of *Ataraxia* delivers the experiencer from the binding tensions of preference that tend to fix the observer into a singular space of having arrived at a perceived truth. The method or details of acquiring the state of Ataraxia is deftly left to the sojourner of truth by Pyrrho; an indication of his uncommon philosophical maturity. The greatest minds in human history know precisely when to stop talking.

Socrates (470-399 BCE) is perhaps the western standard for which all philosophical figures are measured. The venerated Athenian citizen retains all the model characteristics of the legitimately revered sage: Dynamic student progeny in Plato (428-348 BCE) and Xenophon (430-354 BCE); a unique system of existential inquiry (Socratic Method); transcendent ideas that do not conform to traditional zeitgeist of the day; and the trademark feature of being the martyred subject of a death sentence levied by those in social power who felt threatened by the unsettling force of his inner revelations. Socrates was concerned mainly with reconciling the natures of reason and of the divine in men by exploring notions of justice, morality and ethics. Socrates' real genius lies not in his arrival to any particular viewpoint, but in his method of getting there. *Elenchus*' explicit protocol is one of deconstruction, deduction and moral discernment. Though the process appeals to reason, the Logos is dimensionally seductive in that it is the same method used by many spiritual disciplines to arrive at the essence of Being.

Mystics throughout history have offered a unique heritage of philosophical rumination. Mystics embody a marked personal capacity for the examination of spiritual conscience. In almost every case that search is married to divine contemplations that are so intimate and intense, that there often follows a manifestation of epiphany associated with it. The direct experience of mystical states becomes the hallmark of ministerial authority through which these individuals reveal their revelations to the world. Mystics are often qualified historically as theologians (usually posthumously) because their lives tend to be initially dedicated to the study of one or many schools of religious thought. Monasticism is often associated—at some point—with their life journey, as the confines of ritualism seldom serve the larger context of their inquiries or visions. Mystics often offer the best of both worlds, honoring reason and historical traditions that are life serving, while at the same time acknowledging the transcendent, ephemeral and mysterious aspects of existence. This is not to say that the individuals themselves, as vessels of insight and inspiration, are seamlessly occupying perfected expression in the world. As has been said by many an astute historian, "it is best not to confuse the message with the messenger."

Many mystical teachings have remarkable rapport with AFT premise and theory. Indeed, Awareness Field Theory nods respectfully to several of the more notable mystics. A survey of a few of them includes: Previously mentioned Adi Shankara, as well as Julaluddin Rumi (1207-1273 CE), Paramahansa Yogananda (1893-1952 CE), and Thomas Merton (1915-1968 CE). The appreciation stems from observing how these individuals exemplify a remarkable capacity to function within socio-cultural environments while simultaneously conveying transcendent insights of the divine for consideration to the minds of reason. All of them share the common experience of vision, rapture, epiphany or similar spontaneous ecstatic communion with divine Presence—providing them with the key material through which their wisdom is woven.

There have been noteworthy rationalist pioneers who attempted to offer a system based on a way of conscious seeing that is purportedly not colored or diluted by religion, politics or even academic paradigms. George Gurdjieff (1866-1949 CE) and his understudy P. D. Ouspensky (1878-1947 CE) offered a body of work suggesting that there are powers of the "objective mind" whose faculties can govern the "machine" of the human system. The teachings are rationally nuanced attempts for clarity through what I would describe as a psychology of deliberate determinism. However, the force and willfulness of their characters creates an unfortunate cult of personality, a pretense that flags and exposes a distinct flaw in their pseudo-philosophical approach. Theirs were personal fixations that raged against the abominated Ego structure, while simultaneously indulging an almost mythological adoration of the concept of "higher consciousness."

As is the case with most Zoroastrian-influenced religious and philosophical approaches, doctrines of opposing sentiments (good versus evil, ignorant versus enlightened, positive versus negative) ultimately act as a conceptual diversion to the meaningful task of acquiring conscious liberation from the template of thought itself. In the end, such scheming becomes just another intellectually refined, Super-Ego-based aversion to true clarity. An adulation of the "purity of consciousness" and a hatred of the "tyranny of the Ego" are simply two sides of the same coin. Albert Camus (1913-1960 CE) is known to have chastised Lev Shestov (1866-1921 CE) and Soren Kierkegaard (1813-1855 CE) for their sentimentalized

## Philosophy, Consciousness, Spirituality & Self Help

trickery of the mind's chess games with sin and redemption and with truth and darkness, decrying that both of them should have placed their existential ruminations outside of the sophomoric ploys of polarity indulgences, boldly declaring the existential attitude to be "philosophical suicide."

Be it the heaven and hell of fire and brimstone monotheism, or the sin and purity of monastic mysticism; be it the positive or negative spins of the self-help movement, or even the clever "Ego versus self-realization" of contemporary spirituality; the mythical dualities sponsored by the intellectual projections of dark and light are ever the same. We must see deeper. The Roman philosopher-emperor Marcus Aurelius is attributed to have said, "Life is not good or evil, but a place for good and evil." We may well admire Aurelius, and broaden his insight with: *The universe is not this or that, but a place for this and that to occur.* When we obsess over individual aspects in isolation, we will always miss the wisdom of the whole.

Existentialism, and in particular, Friedrich Nietzsche's (1844-1900 CE) version of nihilism, also attempts to cut through the religious and cultural distortions that condition the subjective self. However, the German philosopher's incessant rejection of conditioned norms deepens harshly over his lifetime, eventually reaching a crescendo of totalitarian intensity. What begins as a refined "not this, not this" philosophy of keen discernment inevitably bloats into a ruthless and critical discrimination, morphing him in the end into an agent of brutal cynicism. Ultimately Nietzsche finds himself without any reliable conceptual foundation for the exhausted psyche to land upon. The quandary of such severe and intellectually confined scrutiny is that it can lend itself to a rather critical manifestation of cerebrally-bound claustrophobic rage; a condition which may have certainly contributed to, if not itself defined, the mental breakdown near the end of Nietzsche's life.

These bold pioneers, and a host of their peers, attempted to navigate the uncharted journey of an autodidactic (if not direct) exploration into nuanced existential ruminations, and in so doing certainly have my respect. In appreciating their efforts, we are consistently put on notice that the true way home does not rest with any philosophical regime that lacks the requisite surrender to mystery. A wise humility understands that each journey unlocks its own equation, something we expound upon in great detail in *The 5th Phenomenon*. The primary key exists in the fact that Awareness Field Theory is a fluid art that places subjective consciousness underneath the confusion of the human psyche, a movement that facilitates a genuine realization to full Presence.

**Consciousness**

The field of quantum physics has engaged a marginal conversation around consciousness through more liberal quantum physicist thinkers like David Bohm (1917-1992 CE), John Hagelin (1954- CE), and Roger Penrose (1931- CE). Though such discussions are intriguing, the academic approaches are often misplaced because the analytical trajectory is always moving from physics to consciousness, and not the other way around. This is why academic theories regarding consciousness, and even the speakers themselves, have been criticized sharply by a full complement of their peers. When discussing sentience, theoretical physicists tend to posit ideas that often approach the nature of sentience with existing academic models. This becomes a classic oversight on the part of any theorist that does not recognize that the analytical brain itself is a measuring device, capable only of rendering targeted insights *selected* from the whole. Thought as a system, without impersonal Intelligence influencing its conclusions, inevitably extracts only partial revelations—no matter how sweeping the variables under consideration. These approaches consistently lack the boldness of a pure review of consciousness because they remain tethered to a mind that is shackled in servitude to the sanctioned citations of existing viewpoints within a given academic community mindset.

Scholarly provincial thinking may provide the requisite academic authority that is expected for scientific treatments, but when aimed at ciphering consciousness, the myopic ruminations routinely cause the theory to wax cumbersome and miss the mark. The old pretense of wanting to insulate the theorist from scrutiny with weighted proof that meets the expectation of obligatory peer review, too often occupies the thinker with peripheral concerns that sacrifice a necessary transparency to the penetrating insights that are required to achieve a deeper disclosure of the subject. I would also offer that the laden process itself is less culpable than the pretext of isolated thinking through which it moves—because it is the pretext and not the process that is mostly mitigating the whole veracity of the theories. This last point becomes quite apparent when considering Bohm's graceful posit of the *implicate and explicit orders*. There is an exquisiteness in the elucidations of the *unfolding orders*, which Bohm presents, that becomes slightly wobbled by the unconscious pretext of the author's articulations. Though nuanced, there is a pretense of assertion within his scholarly clarifications that produces an unnecessary degradation to the elegance of the core presumption of his crafted orders. I have always sensed his dialogues as containing the albatross of cautious constraint and containment around his ideas—too deftly handled and managed. Brilliant minds often require liberation from the seduction of their own insights in order to be free enough to be useful to the author after conception.

Roger Penrose has been one of the few modern era academics that allows for the suggestion that consciousness itself could likely be a "non-computational" operation, and has offered some consideration that awareness might exist outside of quantum and state reduction models. This is a very fluid and courageous assertion for a mind attenuated to scientific review. However, Penrose's luminous outlook became a bit colored when in the 1990s—with the assistance of psychologist colleague Stuart Hameroff (1947- CE)—he engaged in research with the aim of discovering the physical properties of the mind (neural correlates) that could theoretically house or give rise to consciousness by determining what molecular structures of the brain might be able to sustain quantum processes. Proceeding with the premise that consciousness itself is a quantum feature, the two researchers offered a theory called Orchestrated Objective Reduction (Orch-OR), which enjoyed some brief intrigue, but also received a summary dismantling at the hands of respected mathematicians and brain physiologists.

The takedown was inevitable, as it would be for any theorist who attempts to derive the source of consciousness from phenomenal content. It is very difficult for science to reconcile, as we do with AFT, that consciousness does not arise from matter. This will always be the bitter pill for the academic world to swallow when it comes to the phenomenon of awareness. For them, if consciousness cannot be reverse engineered, there appears to be no grist for the scientific millworks. The new academic mind will have to find a working rapport between the rational and the intuitive. The best way to receive such insight is to have direct rapport with the Intelligence that moves in awareness fields outside the mind.

Academic treatments around human consciousness rarely feel to me like inspired reflections on the nature of consciousness that are supported in great measure by the direct experience of the speaker. Predictably, there is nearly always a flawed default to the mechanistic analysis of consciousness; or the conversation becomes awkward and strained when the discussion approaches a rational review of the esoteric nature of awareness. Science wants so badly to explain the universe with science only, but if the intellect could explain the entire universe, the human mind alone would have to *be* the entire universe. This is ultimately the Achilles' heel of purely rational inquiry because concepts themselves are only an aspect of totality, just as thought is only an aspect of Awareness.

Yet AFT is an invitation to, and not a dismissal of scholarly approaches. But that invitation brings one merely to the beginning. It is important to understand that the full scope of AFT's reach will only be hinted at in the early stages of consideration. So much more academic discussion will remain to be explored after the basic premise is assimilated. There are also the pseudo-scientifically esoteric notions awaiting AFT elucidations—like Rupert Sheldrake's (1942- CE) *morphic resonance*, the *placebo effect*, Carl Jung's concept of *synchronicity* (a-causal connection), and aspects of extra-sensory perception including intuition, insight, and inspired creativity. All will eventually find a deeper application and meaning with AFT, where currently they enjoy only a marginal legitimacy. Within the more traditional fields, AFT integration will begin to reveal new understandings around long-entrenched limitations inherent in the un-reconciled ("misbehaving" in physics vernacular) aspects of quantum mechanics, while adding more substantive theoretical ballast to classic relativity. Through AFT we will find less mystery and more meaning in speculative postulates such as entanglement theory, the uncertainty principle, wave function theory, and absolute indeterminism.

J. Krishnamurti (1895-1986 CE), though hardly a formal scholar, was an academic figure that spoke into consciousness. Cultivated from a young age by British theosophist doctrine, he was groomed by their organization to become World Teacher for the conjured Order of The Star in the East (OSE). He became, in time, an intriguing light in some circles by virtue of his nihilist reflections regarding the nature of thought in consciousness. Though Krishnamurti eventually eschewed his OSE affiliation, his lifelong message suffers mightily from a pretense of unrelenting assertion that is peculiarly palpable when observing his speaking engagements. There is an odd and unnecessary urgency that foments throughout his almost dictatorial expositions—an impatience that seems to want to hammer the psyche of the listener into "conscious clarity." He sees thought the way modern academics tend to view consciousness—as an epiphenomenal illusion with no causal power. Both views are not only mistaken, but suffer from the same hyper-fixation of scholarly absolutism.

In short, the scholars themselves must become liberated from the box of thought that so often defines their point of view, and move deeper into a clear consciousness that is integrated with awareness of the primacy of Creator Presence. This practice requires a new order of inspired thinkers who can listen through a quality of receptive reflection that reveals coherent intellectual apprehension—humbled and sourced from primordial Intelligence. AFT declares that the new age of scientific understandings around the nature of consciousness will not come solely from the brain of a human, but through luminous, open minds that are attenuated to the order of Presence that created the universe; a movement that transforms rational science into an art of dimensional inquiry.

**Spirituality**

I am often asked, *what is the standard technique for subjective integration of dimensional Presence, and who are the teachers?* In my youth, I was directed to the path of spiritual sages who advocated renunciation for guidance and direction. I remember being referred as a young man to the teachings of the ascetically pragmatic Ramana Maharshi (1879-1950 CE), who advocated that we simply inquire, "Who am I?" until by successive negation, nothing is revealed but the pure awareness of impersonal Being. I had, and still have great regard for Maharshi, but for all his beauty and clarity from the witnessing state, I quickly ciphered that Ramana never really moved as a man of action in the world. He, and other teachers like him, caused me to wonder how one aspiring to this "self-realization" path could conduct themselves as a parent, a spouse, an entrepreneur, or even a political leader? Mine was not the path of renunciation—

I intuitively knew—because I was not a *spiritual* aspirant. I was a *human* aspirant. I needed something more than ascetic examples of austere living to honor my way of moving in the world.

I knew somehow that my journey of consciousness would not be fulfilled to have just tumbled into the absolute while still in a body—and to there remain in contemplative serenity. It is not the zenith of human expression to become benevolently tranquil, but existentially inert. To value transcendent awareness is one thing, but I longed to wear the raiment of the body while moving with dynamic action that is rooted in passionate clarity. This required another order of teaching. Who in history, I wondered, had successfully modeled how the impersonal state can seamlessly influence our lives while engaged in the world of action? Over many years of historical study I began to realize that there were actually very few recorded examples of this kind of life lived. The fact revealed another reality I found difficult to reconcile; so much of the world teachings around spiritual or philosophical wisdom, even some of the most sacredly well-intentioned ones, are astonishingly incomplete. At the threshold of this insight, I also perceived the reason why this was so.

Inside most ontological review lies a terrain of existential pain so vast that nearly always some heroic notion of escape from the confines of the dreaded travails of the body persists. The distress prompts high-minded fantasies of escape that foment profound transcendence myths that take on many shapes. The reverie of Nirvana, spiritual superiority, self-mastery and other states of supposed attainment attempt to give the dreamer hope that they may rise above the perennial stain of our animal existence. I see reincarnation, for example, as another invention of escapism; a belief structure that for many has displaced heaven and hell as the refreshed afterlife *fantasy du jour*. But like all eschatological myths, the notion of reincarnation is simply another offering for the personality structure seeking immortality to subscribe to. Belief in reincarnation, as with all other post-mortem fairytales, is another comforting distraction to the full impact of embracing mortality and other uncomfortable aspects of our existence.

It is a disenchanting affront for the Ego to be apprised that pure Being carries with it absolutely no imprint or residue of a lifetime when an organism dies. There is nothing personal in the absolute, and nothing eternal about the relative consciousness that occupies a body—even though they are one. Repealing the beloved life after death myth shatters the greatest sacred cow ever invoked by humankind—the personal immortality cult. Embracing the truth around the preciously self-deceptive eternal life intrigue of Ego-confined consciousness is another stratum of the deep narcissism we must clear if we are to ever subdue the colossal self-absorption of the psyche.

Much of today's general interest around the subject of consciousness tends to get exploited by trending *socio-spiritual* movements that actually feed off of the psyche's self-centered obsessions. The most contemporarily significant of these unfolded in the latter half of the 20th century. By 1968 an odd hybrid of eastern religious mysticism and the youth counterculture movement in America had emerged. The peculiar pairing blended the West's drug infused social rebellion, and the East's long-established philosophy of temporal transcendence, whose hallmark was one of mystical union with the Godhead. The counter-culture-mysticism amalgam took shape under a variety of spiritually hip names like "cosmic consciousness" or "transcendental meditation." Eastern-cultured gurus and other self-proclaimed spiritual masters responded by crowding the orbit of the West's hungry youth-like satellites junking up the night sky—transmitting a generous broadcast of enlightenment hyperbole. The rebellious, young American culture was happy to devour it all. The drug-enhanced spirituality of the 1960s strongly nurtured notions of Ego transcendence and cosmic bliss states as the zenith of human experience. It also provided a magnificent escape from the existential overwhelm in America induced by a society offering graphic volumes of meaningless violence to its trammeled culture—with no real end in sight.

Today most of the Anglo old-guard psychedelic gurus like Timothy Leary (1920-1996 CE), Allen Ginsberg (1926-1997 CE) and Terence McKenna (1946-2000 CE) are all gone; Richard Alpert, aka Ram Dass (1931- CE) being the only seminal figure still alive today as of this writing. The sad legacy of the eccentric "tune in, turn on, and drop out" ministry, is that it leaves no spiritual or psychologically affirming heritage behind. The psychedelic grifters of the past are no longer held in any serious esteem as major philosophical figures. Furthermore, there are no traces of any current disciples of the spiritual-drug culture that are meaningfully contributing to the philosophical arts or the field of psychology. The stigmatized movement was never grounded in any sober and legitimate depth work within the human condition, and so its history cannot be associated with any credible consciousness work. The stark take-away from that generation's indulgences is that we have learned that drug-leveraged

## Philosophy, Consciousness, Spirituality & Self Help

expansive states are really no more than escapist sideshows, and not relevant to any coherent exploration of awareness.

Today, users of non-pharmaceutical "naturally harvested" drugs sometimes posture that they are "conscious" users, and routinely employ the somewhat tired argument that the ancient shaman or "medicine man" indulged in non-synthesized, organically sourced psychedelics to induce benevolent visions for the people. Aside from the generous dose of historic embellishment proceeding from that premise, there is some veracity to the suggestion that such roles may have been played in tribal cultures—but we may fairly ask, to what end? Where is their wisdom today? In all of history we cannot locate one great historical medicine man or shaman who shook the world, or changed the tide of human affairs with his or her profound drug-induced hallucinations. An Ego, ascribing meaning to psychotropic trips after the high subsides, is hardly a significant contribution to any culture.

Perhaps most noteworthy is the deliberate, but unspoken assertion in all these medicinally leveraged exhortations. It is saying unabashedly that the organic design of human beings is somehow not sufficient to access expansive states without leveraging them with externally acquired and ingested substances. I find it troubling to even consider that the naturally endowed attributes of our species would require that we must alter our brain chemistry to achieve such organic ends as love, peace, clarity, joy and creativity—let alone an evolved consciousness. The pretense of medicinal spirituality within the drug culture has been a lost cause for more than a few generations now—it is time to lay it to rest. So much trendy spirituality erroneously values the transcendent states of impersonal consciousness, feverishly pursuing a desire to acquire or mimic that stillness beyond the subjective self through drugs or pretense spirituality. These have never been complete acts of Presence. Willfully acquiring preferred states of consciousness has always been another escape mechanism for the subjective mind. Clear consciousness work that taps into the depths of our capacity to be fully aware is sober, committed work, and not for the ritual escapist.

It is time for us to find the source of our consciousness by coming naturally to the orders of Presence that we are pointing to in Awareness Field Theory. Having integrated that, we must then return to the body and *live*. The contemplative life must ultimately be supplanted by praxis, evolving into our own unique action in the world. The first movement must be surrender to consciousness without form (Impersonal Being). The second act follows a return to the subjective mind for the computational definitions of an integrated consciousness embodied. This is the seed of wisdom inside the biblical tale of the Prodigal Son: We cannot remain at home in the intellect, subserviently feeding off of ideological doctrines, waiting for the inheritance of dead ideas to give us meaning. We must move out into the unknown with (and beyond) our bodies—in order for us to really come back home and occupy the gift of our mortal endowment.

With current technology has come a brand new challenge. The bulk of human beings now swim in a consciousness of social indoctrination that presses them into a massive, projection-enhanced pseudo-connectivity. Social media has become a paradigm of fragmentation more shocking in scope, and insidiously damaging, than was even the overt glazing of the drug culture generation that preceded it. The *screen-device culture* has become so alarmingly void of

## Philosophy, Consciousness, Spirituality & Self Help

real wisdom, that a renewed embrace of traditional religion has recently enjoyed an almost nostalgic spike in interest. Unfortunately, the recycling of conventional theosophy will simply not serve the current evolutionary requirements needed to achieve the clarity of consciousness that will be necessary to navigate the new terrain of the human condition. Ethical morality, a clever attitude, or even moral turpitude no longer suffices to marshal a new generation's youthful swagger, as has been the case in the past. The playing field is far more complex than it has ever been. Something deeper is required to meet the need. Into that void has stepped the personal empowerment movement.

**The Self-Help Movement**

Starting in the 1970s, new programs would begin to spew forth decades of workshop participants who flocked to them in giddy droves for the "take-control-of-your-life" seminar or retreat. Initially fired by the successes of Werner Erhard's (1935- CE) "EST," workshop attendees would roll out afterward on a mini-high of short-lived self-determination that might last as long as it took for the spell of the facilitator's charisma to wear off. The exploited manage-your-destiny faithful often found that by the time they got home they were strangely miserable all over again—but the die had been cast. The trendy 1980s programs became, in many ways, another non sequitur of positive-vibe acumen, marketed to those seeking a sense of purpose and meaning through the turbo-hyped "philosophy of abundance and control." The self-help surge continues on today, setting its profit margin sights on appealing to the entrepreneurially minded. "Leadership" techniques and "mindfulness" seminars tempt today's fortune seekers to master their destiny in the brave new world. There is an obvious rehashing in these teachings of stale and routine pop-psychology approaches from the past that might be easy to miss if one hasn't been around the block a few times.

The new spin typically attempts to integrate recent studies and research that reveal the latest breaking insights from the neuroscience and neurobiology fields of study. The trending empowerment zeitgeist is pointing to fulfillment that is grounded in a tailored pseudo-science; something that feels a bit less regimented and far more pleasant than the old ego-confronting transformational approaches of the EST-influenced families. But the intent is no more evolved than it ever was in any of these circles. The hip and sexy "body-mind-spirit" approaches are deftly married to financial well-being and "personal growth," with promises of rapid career success just waiting to be harvested by the committed program participant. Cultivating the unbeatable mind, or the mastering of emotions that make for confident business leaders have become ubiquitous slogans on the current workshop circuit with thousands of well-marketed sideshows to wade through. The whole tidal surge has become another moon cycle of personal prosperity intrigue, and in many ways I see it as a kind of corporate cousin to religion and pretense spirituality, offering its own polished version of "heaven on earth."

Where would society stand today if it were to distill out all Ego-sponsored hyperbole of the enlightened self-help movement, along with its belief-entrenched proletariat ally, dogmatic religion? *The 5th Phenomenon* approaches the study of consciousness in ways that avoid the contemporary pitfalls of spiritual escapism and pop-psychology. Ruminations on Awareness Field Theory are simply presented as a proposition regarding the nature and structure of the consciousness we are immersed in as sentient creatures. AFT proffers an understanding that is void of agenda, hype or unnecessary ideological residue. True exploration of AFT has no ulterior motive. Perhaps that is why out of all these forms of teaching, the narrow band of study called phenomenology resonates most to me as an author and a learner of the human condition.

Philosophy is at its best when it finds that edge of wise inference *and* intuitive supposition, seeking content *and* context, micro *and* macro viewpoints, all aimed at reaching broad existential reconciliation through bravely inspired new visions. Genuine noetic review is meant to be a healthy reflection that finds itself transparent to, and in contact with, something larger than the observer. Who will be the next Edmund Husserl (1859-1938 CE), willing to embrace the audaciousness of a transcendental subjectivity— standing with (and not absolute about) his or her worthy insights, regardless of whether or not that understanding were trend-worthy or even empirically provable? My ear has often preferred the unreasonable sage to the prudent theorist. Concerns over reputation or success have no place in a living, fertile philosophy because any vital wisdom will always risk directing us to the mysterious nature of consciousness—and not just the practical or verifiable.

## AFT

Human consciousness engaged in full integration with the complete complement of sentient awareness fields displays something we can only reference in terms of a pure phenomenon that belies any sense of limitation. The intelligence and creative power within the awareness systems that we access approaches the miraculous because those fields source themselves directly back to the Creator. The quality of our performance in this life is directly correlative to one's capacity for individual transparency to the Source Presence described in AFT. Though we must not attribute every aspect of exceptional achievement solely with transpersonal consciousness, it is quite apparent that such occasions always come in intimate association with it.

AFT is not intended to be a guidebook to personal enlightenment, or a doctrine on how to win the race to self-realization. AFT approaches the phenomenon of consciousness as the omphalos of our existence, which we must engage first and foremost with humility, reverence and wonder. The direct experience of these virtues becomes essential before we can embark upon any passionate intellectual inquiry regarding our existence. The sage-poet Rumi says it best with a timeless invitation to "Break the wine glass, and move toward the glassblower's breath." AFT heralds that victory comes to those who with all physical faculties attenuated to the truth of the matter listen without ears, and see without eyes until all utilitarian knowledge recedes into the vast horizon of complete clarity. The true common ground exists beyond the ground itself. Here "…beyond the fields of right and wrong," as Rumi says, "…we shall meet."

An embrace of AFT invites an active availability to Presence that reaches beyond the perceptions of the physical body; a necessary movement toward coherently illuminated consciousness. To highlight this point I will share an experience I had with integrated

# Philosophy, Consciousness, Spirituality & Self Help

Intelligence in action. The instance, interestingly enough, did not involve an experience with our own species, but with dolphins. I was in Cozumel, swimming with these creatures in an area where this was commonly done. At some point two dolphins swam directly underneath my feet and with their rostrum lifted my entire body out of the ocean, swimming underneath me as they carried me along for twenty yards or so. I had been instructed by guides to simply keep my knees locked, and the dolphins would do the rest. So there I was, standing with my feet just skimming the surface of the water, with a dolphin beak supporting each foot. I moved forward across the ocean under their balance support and power—it was an amazing moment. The physical feat of two dolphins, together lifting and transporting 175 pounds of live weight above the waterline is astounding enough, but here is the part that really struck me: I could *sense* their communication. I could palpably feel the intelligence in their actions. There was a marked sense of rapport distinctly moving between their physical bodies that was manifesting the subtle exchange.

These creatures are coherently operating from the open awareness fields described in *The 5th Phenomenon*. The difference for them is that they are not stuck inside the box of thought abstractions. Unlike humans, they do not create subset realities that distract or inhibit their access and integration to open field awareness systems. This species is functioning from the full depth of consciousness available to them. The physiological system of brain activity in these animals is coherently subsumed by the subtler depths of impersonal Presence. I clearly sensed them manifesting a consciousness that was accessing and imparting deliberate understandings without engaging language constructs. Dolphins are famous for benevolent cooperation. They do not utilize spoken language; therefore their consciousness is not corrupted by the conceptual abstractions that crystalize around language. They do communicate physically with "clicks" but the exchanges construct a primarily perfunctory interaction, generated mostly as cues to direct attention to something specific in the physical environment. For these select oceanic mammals the more complex relational exchanges are conducted utilizing open awareness factors accessed and exchanged through an individual consciousness that is transparent to, and immersed in the pure Intelligence of the Creator. Communication without the conflicting distractions of thought-based projections allows dolphins to conduct themselves in a fluid symbiotic rapport with one another. Dolphins (and whales) provide for us an example of extraordinarily intelligent and complex creatures that are engaging the full range of extra-sensory consciousness they are designed to utilize.

People clearly have a different evolutionary legacy than do Cetaceans, if not only by virtue of our capacity for the sophistications of speech. Having developed on land as terrestrial creatures, we adapted to an environment where audible sounds carry with little distortion over significant distances. Unlike underwater conditions, detailed sounds that are uttered on land translate coherently through the gaseous ethers of air. The conditions for humankind were perfect for the specific craft of detailed vocalizations. Complex language, in turn, requires conceptualization and thought abstraction. Unlike dolphins or whales, the language we use has deepened a dimension of complex visualization that we must negotiate within our conscious experience every moment.

a challenge that has developed into the prime obstacle of actualizing clear consciousness within human sentience. We are left to reconcile the trappings of highly complex and explicit thought, symbol and language deliberations with the innate and implicit dimensional rapport of mystical Presence.

What would a fully integrated sentience look or feel like in human beings when manifested? AFT sees it as a marriage between the omniscient Presence of the Creator and a seamless attenuation of individuated consciousness to that noumenal aspect. At this state of our evolution, such achievements in subjective awareness are in fact a fairly rare phenomenon. Varying degrees of integration along the spectrum of sentience are being expressed throughout the general cross-section of humanity. An observation of these gradients of conscious radiance reveal three variables that determine the quality and dimensional reach of actualized human awareness. AFT defines those aspects as *consistency*, *depth*, and *fluidity*.

*Consistency* is the relative proportion of time an individual tends to abide in a state of transparency to the field of Presence, as accessed through the Vig. *Depth* is the individual's scope and capacity for interpreting and ciphering wise perception transmitted through the direct experience of Presence. *Fluidity* is the measure of an individual's ability to adapt, evolve and remain open to Presence during the vicissitudes of circumstance—without letting the pretense of psychic devices sever the rapport of conscious communion. When all three qualities are wholly present in symbiotic harmony, there is an actualization of fully realized dimensional Presence. Most individuals will typically express some varying proportional composite of all three virtues, because complete actualization of the trinity has so far proven to be relatively elusive. This however, *is* the design potential of the human awareness system. Conscious Presence in humans is an art that is meant to denote a beauty like no other life on the planet—and this does not make us superior creatures, it makes us expressly *unique*.

Consciousness of course, is not the sole domain of our species, just as awareness field systems are not limited to living organisms. With AFT we acknowledge Intelligent Presence is everywhere, in all matter, animate and inanimate. Letting go of the tired Cartesian tenant of "I think, therefore I am," opens the door to a humble and coherent approach to the study of the full nature of our sentience.

*The 5th Phenomenon* invites us to accurately reveal the human condition, and further our capacity to function in accord with our organic design. Understanding the way consciousness operates is of critical import as we look at the challenges facing us inside the psychic landscape we must all navigate. For in the final analysis, we, like the dolphins, must cooperate in order to thrive as successful creatures in this world.

Cooperation, to be certain, is the key to any significant change or progress we make on this planet. AFT recognizes that cooperation is derived from a harmonically dimensional consciousness, but some fundamental realizations about human behavior also need to be considered and clarified as well. The most basic principle involves the dynamics around *human motivation*. For human beings to operate in accord with one another, there is always the requirement of solidarity around the motivation that binds them.

On the current scale of the human condition, survival has been the primary, and perhaps most powerful, motivator for solidarity, though certainly not the only one. The most important consideration regarding survival as an essential motivator is that the principle driving mechanism within it is *fear-based*. The significance of all fear-based motivators for humans is that they lack a coherent connection to the full and exact nature of our existence; fear never sees the whole picture. Actions proceeding forth from motivations born from fear in our species tend to elicit distortions that breed violence. War and revolution seldom bring more than a recycled corruption from the last fear-based regime. Such are the poisoned fruits of motives that are driven by fear, no matter how noble the ideological basis.

AFT envisions that human beings operating out of the clarity of Presence that exists prior to the distortions of the psyche, conduct themselves with actions that are not fear-based, and are also free of the personality's enslavement to attraction-aversion polarities. Harmony-derived action has no personality complex residues to mollify it because the vision is whole, and the movement is informed by Creator-Intelligence. Manifesting action out of this state is akin to directing lightening. The creative power of Source moves through us, and we do not attempt to utilize it for any program of individual gain. We cannot know for sure how the transmission of creative force inherent in our directed lightning bolt of consciousness will affect the world around us, but ultimately—when we are clear—this is Life's business, not ours.

I have faith that solidarity of human conduct centered in this kind of consciousness could evolve the race and insulate our world from the dangerous cycles of violence that humans currently perpetrate on nature and each other. AFT confirms that *Consciousness* is the final frontier. There is no other place for us to explore that will endow us with the full understandings we need to actualize our existence and fulfill the magnificent legacy of our species. ✪

## Chapter 14
## Sexuality

It is important to speak into sexuality for so many reasons, and with regard to Awareness Field Theory the subject becomes quite relevant to living a life of general clarity. There is a *prime directive* theme about sexuality in humans. Though every system has its anomalies, most every human has a sex drive. A current population of seven billion people inhabiting the planet suggests the accuracy of that statement. The sexual instinct has a physiological imprint informed through DNA, and is heavily reinforced through culture and its extended social constructs. Along with our basic survival impulse, sex ranks as one of the top two physiological drivers.

But sex is unique, in that parts of the brain reinforce and reward its behavior with significant doses of biological chemicals that induce pleasure factors in the body. The variety and volume of chemicals released during sexual activity is a drug cocktail worthy of any pharmacist's arsenal: Twenty different types of endorphins including dopamine and acetylcholine, hormones such as adrenaline that boost performance, and pain blockers like oxytocin. During sexual activity the body increases endorphin production specifically on average 200%, and it's an experience that the mind does not forget. Easily the most physiologically pleasing activity, it stands to reason that sex compels a great deal of attention.

Adding to the momentum of biological drive and pleasure center rewards, human cultures generally celebrate interest in sex, arguably to the point of obsession. A predictable exploitation of sensual allure has taken hold, and morality-based restraint tactics offer very little current against the massive tide of hypersexual predilection. In short, sex is a place where we have become quite lost. So what is healthy sex? What can we identify as truly clear sexual expression? To explore such a personal, yet human-wide activity with accuracy requires a candor and depth of wisdom that is commonly lacking in current social discourse around the subject.

AFT offers a look at sexuality from a viewpoint that is larger, and therefore more complete than the limited scope of typical discussions around physiological sex. Awareness Field Theory allows us to review the act of sexual expression without being held captive by the physical or psychological experience, so that we can deeply explore the subject with clarity. That being said, this approach will not be a treatise laboring over notions of sexual self-mastery. Nor will the exploration produce a program, ritual, or sect of spiritual sexuality that would propagate some Ego-laden notion of how to be a superior lover. A look at sexuality through the lens of AFT will endeavor to see the subject more comprehensively through the various systems of consciousness.

## Sexuality

Tantric doctrines promulgated around esoteric sexual practices offer a typical "spiritual" glazing of the carnal act, while never really touching the deep wisdom available in sex. Most likely the trend has its roots in the Buddhist "left-handed" path of Vajrayana. Yet, in spite of being couched as a path to enlightenment, tantra models focus on the physiological acts of sex, with a distinctly Western Ego-generated emphasis on willful control regimes designed to direct sexual energies in the body, or to enhance pleasure or stamina. This focus is not about clarity within conscious sexual expression, nor does it address the *full* potential in sexual rapport. The teachings may offer the appearance of being evolved, but the pleasure principle espoused is obvious, and for the sincere aspirant, the sensuality loop ultimately fails to fulfill. True sexual communion also requires lovers that are deeply bonded. Profound depths of sexual rapport are simply not available between transient paramours or sex surrogates and clients.

Communion through sexuality is an area of human exploration that is barely dawning. I see this arena as essential to an evolution in consciousness, because the openness and honesty that manifest during clear and present sexual exchange innately draws upon the virtues of trust, humility, and passion; all qualities that invite a clarity of Presence that promotes healthy relational intercourse in general. As we explore sexuality with an AFT perspective, we forgo the distractions of the "great sex/great lover" narrative that is commonly engaged around the subject. I see more profound possibility in a clear examination of sexual potentials than I do in establishing high-minded sacred sex protocols that we might all aspire to in order to project some sense of imagined virility in our lives. Instead, with AFT we are looking for an honest reconciling of what is happening within these intimate exchanges to determine what is fully available to us with regard to sexual communion.

I find it is essential to approach the subject of sex with a basic understanding: Sex requires openness—both physically and emotionally. Yet, in sexuality there is another aspect of receptivity rarely discussed or wisely explored. It is an AFT feature known as *Dimensional availability*, and it is essential to having a complete experience during physical communion. This availability has to do with the quality of each lover's individual consciousness, and not about the usual (physiological) chakra or prana energy dynamics often referred to in the various Tantric contexts. With AFT, we are addressing the awareness field rapport that exists between two lovers as they come together physically for sexual exchange, and referring to it as "dimensional availability." For myself, sex before the exploration of this work had no mutual awareness around the real quality of consciousness that my partner and I were manifesting as we moved into sexual intimacy.

What is meant by the "quality of consciousness" in this context is the nature of the full complement of self-awareness systems as they engage in sexual exchange. In review of these systems with regard to sexual encounters, one might ask the following questions. Within each individual, is there a clear personal consciousness that is manifesting *agenda-free attention*? In addition to each individual's clarity, is there available an open transparency of each lover to the other—is the posture of *receptivity* mutual and pure? Most significantly, is there a third intangible element of *stillness* that the two individuals are swimming in at communion? The attribute of this third ingredient is something that most lovers are wholly unfamiliar with. The element of stillness during sexual exchange is essentially a crucible of impersonal Presence that embraces and infuses the relational aspects of the subjective lovers as a co-mingling residue. This sexual trinity creates an integrated experience of subjective communion—one approaching the mythological state of unity consciousness.

Rapport as realized through sexual intimacy is profound. A less physically and emotionally intimate variation of this quality of relational exchange represents the purest form of communication that is available to us. In other words, remove the sex and retain the rapport, and we have the deepest, clearest, and highest expression of platonic interaction possible. Relational affinity of this order is an important piece for our evolution. It may seem ironic to consider that the key to finding meaningful platonic connection with others could arise from an art discovered through exploration of sexual intimacy with our beloved. I maintain that the greatest success we might know in working together as a people could be contingent on our ability to achieve the highest design potentials in our sexual expression. Perhaps this is why we commonly refer to the venue of healthy sexual rapport as *lovemaking*.

Of course, much of the difficulty around achieving fully realized sexual rapport arises when our subjective consciousness becomes saturated with the enthralling conditions of our physiological experience. The possibility for genuine sexual intimacy in these instances unfortunately devolves into an intense habit of escape from self-intimacy. When our attention is taken captive for the purposes of intrigue-based erotica, we produce and compel agenda-oriented intercourse.

The continued intrusion of thought into well-intentioned sexuality can be problematic for many who embark on an exploration of the clear act of sexual congress. Years of conditioning around the carnal aspects of sex often will produce the deeply entrenched sexual images and concupiscent ideas that haunt attempts at the more organic sexual expressions that exist at deeper levels. A sudden or spontaneous commitment to healthy sexual intimacy does not always bring immediate cessation of these old programs, because they are so reinforced by years of the pleasure-centered conditioning that have accompanied them. Often it will take months, or even years of what might feel like a decompression of sorts, as the body/mind becomes accustomed to the more subtle aspects of dimensional lovemaking.

It will take time for the thought-based reactivity of sexual exchange to begin to fade because the mind will be habitually searching for "ground" on which to commence with its lustful protocols. The Ego-based sense of a subjective self will try to impose projections upon the moment in order to create the requisite sense of *tension in opposition* to the sexual partner through objectification. When seen in this way, we begin to understand just how superficial and unconsciously calculating most human sexual exchange often is. Orgasm is one aspect of performance that is almost always expected by one or both partners. Emotional affirmation is another personality demand that is also typically desired and expected. When there are a multitude of motives around sex, the movement is always from the mind, even if feelings of affection and caring are mixed in. Stated another way, sex has become an intoxicating act of acquisition, and not a movement of receptivity and communion with another. Acquisition requires a mind-oriented strategy that utilizes sex as an intense distraction from genuine self-intimacy, while communion necessitates a clear openness and availability to one's self and partner.

Curiosity can help us break free. Curiosity in this context means a desire to openly explore receiving our partner without any subjective evaluation of what we are experiencing. The act becomes a direct reception of our lover with only the intent to connect and commune. This is an art that occurs when the receiver is not *accumulating* any of the experiences exchanged during the receptive act. As the movement becomes more and more fluid, sexual rapport becomes sublime, alive and without boundary. Expressing intimacy in this way, we find possibilities moving well beyond any expectations we have been accustomed to in typical lovemaking.

Sexuality is so very physical, and though we are genetically hardwired for the perfunctory task of procreation, the deeper dimensional expression referred to in *The 5$^{th}$ Phenomenon* will eventually require us to cultivate a new order of Presence in love-making that organically runs deeper than conditioning and instinct. AFT invites us to consider that sex is where the act of physical intimacy becomes a realization of the full potential of human relational capacities. This is how sex becomes a living art that conceives love, *before* it considers conceiving children. ✺

# CHAPTER 15
# Love

The mind is a huge wall tagged with an epic volume of graffiti, and love is the endless space on either side. In this world, the most beautiful and profound love tears the heart from the chest, and shatters the mind to stillness. We should have it no other way. Love beckons us to unreasonable passions, to endure the inevitable agony of perceived separateness and loss—acts that will forever brand our heart with the ultimate symbol of love: Fire.

Like fire, love consumes us. Yet without it, nothing changes, nothing new grows. Without love there is no relationship, no creation, no life. When we truly love, everything must die that would prevent us from sincerely touching Life. Again and again, we are compelled to act outside reason, sacrifice beyond our own self-preservation and give until we are spent. The most compelling feature in existence makes absolutely no sense. That is because love is from elsewhere. Love is the cherished guest in our home who makes us aware that we too are from some other world. And if we truly receive that message, we realize that we must one day journey back to that other place, to dwell again among the tribe of our true origin.

Contrary to so much dramatic emphasis, love is not an emotion. In Awareness Field Theory, *love is the first movement of creation*, and it will be the last movement of its closure. Underlying the core equation of the cosmos is the master element of love. In silence, and only in silence, is the sublime element of Creator love *fully* received. Creator love reveals the great benevolent Intelligence to the able perceiver in waves of epiphanies that have no beginning and no end. For any self-aware creature, core redemption arrives the very moment that we occupy the love that created us. That act becomes fulfilled through the intimate journey of the body.

Accessing Creator love has always been the most passionate route to clarity. The keynote requirement to be taken by the pure Love Path is unleashing the radical tenderness that dissolves us into the sublime realm. Because love is the primordial creative element, with it, nothing is impossible. This is the authoritative passion of the transformative Christ that represents the closest tonal attribute we have to the human experience of intimacy with the Creator. Christ's journey and fate are all about the full expression of devotion to the Creator as Beloved, but achieved through profound *self-intimacy*. The Christ figure surrenders all to the Master Intelligence, and in so doing is released from all distortion of rational existence. His acts are so deeply rooted in pristine Noumenal Presence that we can feel the immediacy of his love sending transmissions in human potential down through the ages.

Thus we see that the artfulness of Jesus' devotion to life is not transcendence-based. It manifests as a potent contrast to the liberation platform of many spiritual figures. Christ's ministry is fervently of the body, even though his "kingdom" is not ultimately defined by the phenomenal world. He intimately relates through the instrument of his body while seamlessly bathing in deep Presence. As a result, his existence exudes compassion, humility, *and* ferocity. He moves deliberately through the corruption and bias of human affairs, and while his clothing may become blemished with the mud and blood of an unconscious mankind flanking him, his heart remains diaphanous, numinous and unstained. Through it all he allows himself to be accessed, even as he himself reaches out to make connection. He does not isolate in the ivory tower of the enlightened witness. Above all claims made for him as an epic life teacher, Jesus is a true master of the potent path of love.

Such love in action is not distracted by the whirlwind of the mind. Love is not fixated with reason or logic, memory or time, or any of the myriad fascinations of matter it occupies. It has but one directive everywhere it abides: Express the *Tao* as realized through relational intimacy. Through the Tao of the Creator, we become a precious aspect of the sacred communion that emanates from Source. As we become still inside, we find a return to the primary AFT axiom underlying existence: *Love is the first and primary movement of creation.*

Love is the most intimate experience we can have with the great Source of all things while embodied, and it is ultimately beyond description. My wife is fond of referring to this sublime sense of love as "stillness in motion." The essence is ever alive, without floor, wall or ceiling. In the end, love becomes a release into a beautiful clarity so sublime that it is *nearly* unbearable to embody. In this way love abides as an exquisite respiration of Being; a tenderness that inhales into the very heart of surrender, married to a grace that exhales out as the primordial impulse of creation.

Between individuals, relationship becomes the spawning ground of love because relational exchange is the primary operational component of the cosmos. A universe of absolute unity commands no interaction, but the diversity of our cosmos mandates it. Everything that exists is performing as an aspect of relationship. Within human sentience, relationship between emotionally bonded creatures actualizes a harmonic expression that comprises the alchemy of love.

Mankind's romantic *idea* of love is anemic by comparison, often presented as merely a contrasting subset to the human capacity for apathy. Heroic notions of love become projections that tend to reduce love to the conceptual foil for hate or cruelty. Such versions of love simply do not exist outside of the generation and perpetuation of these concepts within the human mind. Investment in them becomes escapist, and yet another false pretense that obfuscates a direct experience of the genuine expression of love.

The love of the Creator is a living universal phenomenon, infused in the very fabric of all awareness fields. This actualization of love is sourced from the primordial emanations of the Creator itself, transcendent of and prior to, any individual human experience. Italian poet Dante Alighieri (1265-1321 CE) addresses the matter of *divine love*, born from the "Heavenly Rose of Light," in the sweeping *Commedia*, completed in 1320 CE. Dante describes this ultimate intimacy as "…the love that moves the sun and other stars." Love realized in this context has little to do with the sentimentalities of affection that are mere ruminations of the personality structure. Actual love is experienced as a living communion between those whose bond is rooted deeper than matter, time and space. Such bonds of love often manifest themselves in metaphysical ways, defying all rational explanation.

This is why "psychic" stories between lovers are not uncommon. You may very well have a few of your own. Open connections of love utilize consciousness fields that are acutely transparent to one another, and much like notions of quantum entanglement in physics, any act commenced by one party immediately affects the field of the other regardless of the space between them. Entanglement Theory itself is predicated on the notion that *relationship* is the defining factor of everything in the universe. In AFT, entanglement scenarios within the context of physics occur because the superposition state is involved with more than one particle, essentially forming a relational triangulation of mutually open influence. AFT purports that vector exchanges between the awareness fields of human bonds robustly mirror the dynamic expressions of entanglement theory, and arise as an outcome of the alchemical algorithms of awareness field interactions that are fundamentally comprised of Love. Presence is the only ubiquitous phenomenon in all the cosmos, and the bonds of love perform under the direction of its lawless essence.

Creator love is the ultimate determinant for the absolute realization potential of all living things, and is the zenith of our expression as sentient creatures. Love beckons all to the last great act of deliverance, a journey that takes us back to the Source that authored the Elysium of totality. Love is designed to be a facet that colors sentient life, because love can potentially liberate consciousness by becoming a transcendent constituent to the prime existential directive of all living things: The instinct to survive. This is why *life* and *love* are so intimately related.

Since its inception, scientific thought has debated how to define life. Trite details around cell division, capacity to grow, reproduce, or even the ability to regulate organism temperature all have been offered as definitions for what constitutes life. However, the answer is very simple from an AFT standpoint. A living thing is that which consciously responds to its environment with a self-sustaining protocol. Every living creature's prime directive is to survive and perpetuate itself as a coherent system; therefore if that system interacts with its environment in such a way that its actions cause it to preserve (or grow/evolve) the state of its existence, then it is alive. All life is wired to survive, and a human being's survival instincts are the most fundamental and basic of all motivational drivers. There is only one thing we know of that overrides the survival instinct: Love. I find this epiphany to be a significant revelation to our evolution because it is the most direct way out of the darkness within the human condition. Love is, in fact, the salvation of *any* creature that biologically evolves to the point of conscious self-reflection.

When love releases us from the yoke of an existence predicated solely on survival, it transforms a myopic sentience into a state of awareness that senses and moves from something larger than just self-serving instincts. But we can only embrace and preserve this level of love by consciously surrendering to a more profound act than self-preservation. As love releases us from the slavery of an existence relegated only to survival, it simultaneously delivers us from the bondage of fear associated with it. This movement foretells the end of all violence, and the beginning of the final order of human unfolding and expression.

It bears repeating, *love is the first movement of creation, and it will be the last.* Any aspect of existence that ignores this fundamental truth will suffer, and violence will follow until the error is reconciled. This is the "subtle pretext of purely mortal error" that my first consciousness teacher, Alice, spoke of. For human beings, there is this fundamental forgetting that the aspect of love is the Source and foundation of our existence. This lack of awareness has caused us to lose the precious art of being in direct and seamless relationship with the Creator. We have become estranged from our living bond to the Genesis of all things. Perhaps by innocent mistake, we are asleep to our full nature—unaware that the most immediate way out of the dream of separation is through intentional re-immersion into the phenomenon of love that can awaken us. AFT invites human beings to cross the threshold of separation and fear, and return to the love that Sources all, so that we may re-occupy our place in the essence of its sublime body. From there we may reconsider our perceptions of the world, and finally come to move in truth, clarity and passion. ✣

# CHAPTER 16
## The Lens

When I was in college studying the craft of filmmaking, I remember being shown an old-time movie camera from back in the first days of the industry. Those original motion picture recording devices were clunky and cumbersome instruments. The one I am recalling had an interesting detail on it. The face of it was equipped with several rotatable lenses that could be dialed in over the shutter portal that led to the chamber where the film was exposed. This was a clever instrument for its time because it manually allowed for a quick and easy interchange of lenses that could create varied exposures on the film. A lens on a camera controls how the film receives the outside world. In later decades, more sophisticated lenses would further enable the user to control how reality was recorded.

Along my journey I have observed how the thinking mind creates a lens between the world and what we perceive. The mind shapes and defines what is received through our senses (like what gets exposed on film) and then fabricates stories around those perceptions. The need to have one's self-generated viewpoints be accepted and approved of by others is an immediate dilemma for the personality structure because it creates a field of tension, while simultaneously setting a tone of expectation around all relational experiences with others. Without Presence abiding as the crucible of our sentience, the wayward psyche yearns to present itself as compelling and relevant to the world—almost as if to compensate for the missing integer of Presence in its overall content.

In my life there were two initial instances where, by grace, the lens of my thinking mind was for a time completely removed, allowing me to be free of the aforementioned anxiety. Both occurrences came on the heels of a mental suffering so intense that it created an actual sensation of heat inside my head that felt unbearable. The spontaneous and radical removal of my mind's processing filter produced an immediate sense of qualitative ease—stillness so untouchable, and so profound—all my psychological anguish completely vanished. These windows of release from all psychic bondage were however, temporary states (the first occasion lasting about eight hours, and the second instance about three months). The significance of the events taught me that my fabricated thinking was not the fundamental reality I had taken it to be for so long. I discovered that my prior perceptions had simply been an interpretation of circumstances based on the conceptual lens I was looking through at the time. Up until that first opening, I had been taking those psychic evaluations to be my *moment-to-moment reality*.

On the event of the first opening, I took notice that though I was still fused with my subjective consciousness, the shift in awareness brought about a condition of experience whereby all my perceptions no longer had a *story* attached to them—I saw everything without evaluation. That initial opening was incredibly liberating, but the second shift was even more profound. The second rupture into clarity would propel me entirely out of the bindings of subjective consciousness and fully into the witnessing state. Many consciousness teachers I had known through the years referred to similar instances they had experienced as a kind of "seeing through" certain thoughts—but in the case of my second shift, I was seeing through the whole *mechanism* of the process of thinking. I could clearly delineate the intellect as a system that possessed its own order and boundary, but at the same time the mind was generating a product of no substantive content. Conceptual reality was a mirage.

I would later cipher that the openings I experienced were an expansion of consciousness into a realm of objective seeing—a release from the bondage of thought-based reality. However these states were not an *organically ripened arrival* to a place of fully integrated clarity of consciousness. The flash-pass liberation from concept-bound sentience had come as a radical and sudden departure from intense, mind-induced suffering. The instantaneous shifts had not manifested as an evolved dimensional clarity over time. Full integration for me would come gradually, deepening over a period of years. The second temporary window of *release as-a-state*, interestingly enough, would eventually collapse into the severest wormhole of dark despair and depression I have ever known—a journey out of which I wrote my first book, *Razing Men*. There are sound reasons why these initial bursts into impersonal awareness fields are worth taking some time to relate, and since the second instance was dimensionally deeper, I will reference that occurrence specifically.

Sparing all the dramatic personal details of an intensely difficult time in my life, I will just relay that one day I broke down to a degree and depth of psychological undoing I had never previously experienced. This condition induced a level of impairment that was unprecedented for me. I found, to my utter dismay, that for two days I was not functional—I never left my bed. However, a radical shift to a new order of awareness occurred immediately upon awakening on the third morning. It was in that moment that I experienced a vast lucid field of awareness where all thoughts were seen to be fundamentally empty of any true content; I extrapolated that thinking had been the real source of all my unnecessary suffering. I witnessed each and every thought now as a little bubble rising to the surface of my awareness and then "popping" into nothing. I saw these "thought bubbles" as stories only—a mere fabrication of the mind. I did not differentiate between good thoughts as valid and bad ones as problematic. I saw them all as equally false. It is an understatement to say that every thought was just a lie; for in that moment I was seeing the whole process of isolated thought as not a *complete truth*. I would later discover that whenever the system of thought is not bathed in Presence, the movements of the mind are rendered incomplete by default.

Upon this second opening, there was an immediate recognition of the basic deception underlying all *fragmented* thinking, no matter what the quality of thoughts. This new awareness shift put my consciousness in a fresh context. I found myself grounded in an expansive stillness, and that vantage point gave me a radically clear view of the operations of the mind. I also sensed that this place of *stillness* was where Being sourced itself from—it brought me to a portal that led to a witnessing state that was completely outside of the subjective consciousness that moved inside the machinations of the body. I saw that I was stillness *amidst* the cacophony of thought. My response to this larger opening was to remain grounded in this clear silence and completely divest all interest or energy in the contents of my mind. There was some sense of urgency around this newfound liberation from the tyranny of incessant thinking, and it fostered an immediate valuing of it above all else. A kind of ruthlessness ensued in which I found that I could actually dismantle every mental notion at its inception with the power of the clarity that was seeing through it. For a good period of time I utilized that power to obliterate nearly all arising thought.

These examples of breakthroughs into witnessing awareness may provide a valuable touchstone toward an individual's evolution of conscious unfolding, but such vapid occurrences are not full integrations of Presence—and the two cases I am referring to, in retrospect, were definitely not absolute arrivals to mature depth consciousness. Abiding in (and sustaining) genuine clarity is a process developed through time according to the distinct algorithms of each individual's consciousness. It is not established by the imposition of extreme experiences, nor is it a derivative of a driving personal will, intense longing, or any other force of human personality. The releases I have described were more like grace intervening with a kind of spiritual triage to palliate excruciating mental anguish. Mature Presence, on the other hand, does not arrive as a relatively distinguished property until real clarity is earned from the practiced art of operating out of a subjective awareness that is consciously integrated into Being—not just a temporary witnessing state induced by some intensely leveraged psychological condition.

Just as many of history's existentialists saw the futility of mind but were never able to see beyond it, so too can a neophyte to the awakened state of witness-to-clarity stall. This spiritual torpor can prevent individuals from getting beyond the initial opening that sees isolated thinking as incomplete. To see that one is not thought is just a sophomore stage of unfolding consciousness. The new clarity must continue its marriage relationship with the body-mind without divorce, deepening until the Absolute integrates all into a complete expression of humanness.

There was another interesting point regarding the second opening. I discovered that along with the new objective distancing from the process of thinking, the personal identity of "Robert Revel" had also faded away by extension, having sourced itself in concept as well. With clarity brought to the faculties of thought, the sense of someone personally acting dissolved. This is a tricky place, because the motivation that one typically uses to manage behavior as the doer is now gone. My usual management and routine decision-making protocols suddenly evaporated. Even the strong motivators of fear and desire were no longer compelling, as there was no sense of any personality showing up to sponsor the emotions. This was not apathy as much as it was a kind of lucid detachment from a lifetime of personal orientation. Yet oddly enough, many of the old tapes of the mind remained somehow intact.

The residual conditioning that was once a product of personal 'doer-ship' continued to present itself to the witnessing state. I observed these habitual programs display themselves in cyclical fruitless patterns, like a tired flow of repeating screen saver images on a computer monitor that no longer capture or engage our attention. The Intelligence abiding within the open field of pre-thought awareness could now advise my actions, and could do so without distraction from the now unconvincing sideshow of my personal conditioning. I was at last established in an understanding that only comes from the influence of Presence that exists prior to thought. This state of clear consciousness became a powerful touchstone that suggested the possibility of a more profound order of functionality in human conduct. Indeed, that radical clarity, and all the evolutionary possibility it points to, has become the primary subject of this book.

Eventually over time, there became a sense that the only real value of personal consciousness rests in moving into each moment in such a way that we are marrying the Intelligent Silence itself to the psychic condition of the body. However, one's adeptness at subsuming psychic structures with Silence is an unfolding process, and the rate of maturation is relative to the depth of ones prior habituation to the dream-state of conceptual consciousness. To challenge the Ego's formidable subjective paradigm, one must possess a strong propensity to access and integrate the stillness of Being. This physical intimacy with the Intelligent Silence beyond personal identity showed me what clear consciousness really is—and I came to cherish it more than anything. The ensuing sense of tranquil depth drew forth in me a chord of ruthless integrity that served to attenuate my attention to what is true when anything but pure clarity moves a body-mind. Intelligent Presence is woven into the fabric of the universe, and that quality illuminates us not through action itself but through stillness amid action. This is also why the subtle nature of Being is so easy to miss—it does not insist on impressing us. The months spent gliding the updrafts of the witnessing state were a delightful departure from the grinding decades of ego-based living, but because creation establishes no permanent promotion to the rank of enlightenment, my precious spontaneous shift was destined to slip away.

As I have mentioned, my three-month long state of serendipitous clarity was only a temporary window, yet the whole experiential sequence provided significant movement in my personal evolution. Before the shift, various teachings around consciousness had suggested that the conditioning of the mind was a problem. Immediately following the shift to the radical witness, my conditioned mind seemed to me to be more of an incidental curiosity than anything else. But in due course, the subjective mind did manage to re-establish a foothold, and this time it came back with a vengeance.

The return to subjective ground was inevitable because I found that the transcendent state was not necessarily ideal for moving in the world socially—or passionately. My life had always lent itself to creative endeavors and self-generated enterprise, and the aloofness of the witnessing state belied the sensual activation of someone personally engaged in productive action. Intensity had always been a hallmark trait that I had utilized to express my range of being human. So as I began to re-occupy my subjective core, and move again with color in my day-to-day affairs, the psychic structure came howling back, hungry to re-establish itself after having been for a time banished to oblivion by the impersonal witnessing state. My Ego regained some of the real estate it had lost and retook the high ground, feverishly fortifying itself against Presence. My returning "personal self" was not the same however, as it was before the openings. It had seen too much, and somehow knew its glory days had passed, and that its current days were numbered. The desperate and final siege of the subjective self began, and the next fifteen months took me to the edge of my capacity to cope with my existence.

My mind went epically out of control. It would rail on non-stop, twenty-four hours a day, seven days a week, like a train that kept roaring through my head without pause or end. There was no escape from the noise, and the sanctuary of the "witnessing state" seemed wholly unavailable to me. My psyche was incessantly plagued with waves of fear, dark thoughts, self-doubt, and an emptiness that was so disturbing that every moment I wondered if I could bear it a second longer. The vicious psychic assault felt utterly apocalyptic, and it seemed to have a bottomless arsenal of ammunition at its disposal. It took me hostage, tore me up, and completely wore me out. Nothing, and no one could help me. Somehow I mustered enough tenacity to refuse all advice or suggestion for the use of psychotropic prescription drugs, which friends and colleagues were urging me to consider as a means to "stabilize" my situation. That I would endure this through my own organic process was the only thing I knew for sure.

Eventually I came to the breaking point, but instead of the expected crash and burn, something unprecedented for me occurred—I totally let go of all my *resistance* to what was happening. I stopped trying to control the outcome, and instead handed everything back to the Intelligence that designed me. Why not let the God that created this situation work it out? I was done, and I didn't care anymore to be the sovereign ruler of my destiny. I was finally over my desperate search to find a solution for meaning, purpose, peace, happiness and even my sanity. For the first time, it didn't matter to me if I lived or died. I didn't actually want to die, I just stopped *fighting* to survive—and there is a key difference. That was the beginning of the end of my unnecessary suffering in this world. That moment became the true start of living a life of freedom through conscious clarity. At long last, I simultaneously realized *and* accepted that I had never really been in control of anything in life—I had just participated somehow in the flow of it. I have been cultivating that insight ever since.

Years later I would look back in reflection and wonder just how or why the ego structure managed to come back even after I had seen that its basic substance—the entire system of thought—was so clearly a fabrication. By the time I found myself seriously pondering the question, the answer came to me directly on the heels of the inquiry. I saw that the experience of seeing through the nature of thought from the witnessing state had not been enough. The necessary element of legitimate transmutation would be brought about in the end by an *intimately direct and complete experience of the utter futility of my psychic structure trying to function separately from Presence*. This, in turn, was followed by a conscious movement of surrender of the allotment of my subjective sentience to the living mystery of Noumenal Awareness. I could now see that with my earlier ruptures into the impersonal, the *witness* was not married to the *actor*.

## The Lens

While this deeper release yielded a new order of transparency to Presence, it did not deliver me to any place of arrival or attainment—as had been the promise of so much spiritual doctrine. However, from that day forward my actions were born of a fuller response arising from the entire estate of my endowed sentience. I still retain the ongoing subjective choice of whether to proceed in service to life or to abuse the conscious station of grace that has become available to me. In my experience, this is what nearly every "realized" teacher either failed to—or was not willing to—communicate. The Absolute Intelligence does not impose *any* state of liberation or enlightenment that permanently binds individual consciousness to a sustained conduct of purity. In addition to this omission from celebrated teachers, I found that the mystical scriptures had also largely betrayed my trust in their doctrines of attainment—The Holy Grail turned out to be a *verb* and not a noun. The whole movement of conscious unfolding has been about riding the edge of radical freedom *and choice* all along—not permanently arriving to some elevated state. The "goal" I had been seeking was the marriage of a precarious subjective sentience to the implicit and sublime influence of Presence. Yet a marriage is not a prison—one can always stray. This order of honesty, humility and accountability appears to be quite difficult for many self-proclaimed "masters" to honestly acknowledge and embody. They can be recognized by the smell of their pretense.

From that first day of surrender, I committed to listen deeply to whatever Creator Intelligence was moving me to do, or not do. The contract required only that I receive Presence and respond out of the organic fidelity that naturally occurred from that position of transparency. I was no longer preoccupied with listening solely to the manic personal self, or the inverse—of soaring above it all—unaffected in the witnessing state. I could now, with depth consciousness, attenuate to impersonal Intelligence and move in the world with the clarity and ferocity I was designed for. That is why everything changed. My thoughts could now be organically utilized to function in *service* to Life, and the pure Presence I was bathing in soothed the chaos of the psyche instantly. What is more, I had finally become a willing agent to the Creator itself, which I found to be an incredible relief. I was no longer a slave to my passions and fears. The journey of fluid awareness continues to unfold and the practice of that art only deepens over time.

It sometimes strikes me as odd that the epic struggles early on with my Ego did not ultimately bring me to a place of desiring an absolute transcending of the thinking mind once I had leveraged my way out of it. Today, I recognize the movement of thought as a necessary and valuable component of our individual expression in the world. I still see how that sense of separate self occasionally moves to resist experiencing the full scope of subjective consciousness, including the Silence from which it arises. Such distortion is no longer a compelling aspect to my existence, but I do still see the mechanism at work inside myself. I understand intimately these prolific resistances to life, the Ego's aversion to full clarity, and the old haunts of the limited mind that tenaciously protest the full content of consciousness—like a minority member wanting to table a committee motion to escape it all.

To exist is to feel these pushes and pulls. To *be* in form is to experience the tension *of* form. For even the tiniest particle of the cosmos there is no escape from the influences of other particles, forces and energies. Our complex mind is no different. It will always have some *ideas* about how it is moving, or how it would prefer to move in the world—what it likes and what it does not. In one sense there is no absolute peace we can attain while simultaneously embracing this existential tension. Even the balance and order of the Tao finds its harmony through a reconciling of natural forces (and polarities) in opposition. Neither contradictory forces nor the harmony of the Tao are absolute states; they are, in fact, meaningless without each other. The only way to reconcile the endless contradictions, polarities and randomness that make up the full dimension of our consciousness is to become seated in that which is prior to manifestation and marry all our existential aspects together on the altar of Being. Here is where the reconciliation of our life's journey begins by affirming our conscious connection to Creator Presence. That experience is not only transcendent and eternal, it is also unambiguously intimate and utterly immediate. It is *intimate* because we directly experience no fundamental separation from the ineffable aspects of our nature. It is *immediate* because Presence preempts all relative states including the projections of time.

Upon awakening to one's full dimensional nature, the illusion of a separate self will gradually loosen its hold when it is seen for what it is. But within that free sense of open awareness, discordant residue can remain within subjective consciousness. Persistent resistance to the expanded state at this phase, however, is no longer perceived as just a device of the separate self. The machinations of the personal psyche are clearly understood to be part of the

Creator's design algorithms that are ripening through consciousness. Willful determinations in the new order of awareness have now been supplanted with surrender to Being. One may be open and fluid—but not insouciant. The operations of the mind here are influenced significantly by the impersonal, but not in a predetermined way. Personal rhythms are accepted and experienced as existential tension manifested by the epic Intelligence of the Creator itself. We discover that we *can* maintain clarity in the storm *without* willfulness.

There is tremendous value in experiencing the varying textures of life through a preserved clarity of consciousness. It is important that we continue to deepen our understanding around the many aspects of distortion within the human condition no matter how evolved we become, just as it is important to keep the knife-edge sharp in the kitchen. Living out of clarity means we have the opportunity to participate in the process of Silence waking itself up to its own design potentials in consciousness. The gift of genuine clarity sees that "no one" is personally doing any of this unfolding. My first attempt at surfing off the coast of California taught me very quickly that it's always the wave that *takes you* for a ride, and not the other way around.

Ultimately we come to realize that the Creative Intelligence is allowing itself to become lost in certain aspects of its own creation. This I take to be the most sweeping expression of non-tyranny, made by the only true power in the universe that could fully impose it. The Creator *allows* confusion and error rather than levying a mandate of permanent bliss and benevolent clarity over all of creation. Human beings are not compelled to conform to some fiat of ethical conduct by God; the creature is designed to be radically free and allowed to arrive at potential through its own deliberations. Interestingly enough, in a relative world, this is the very altar upon which existentialists and agnostics have argued either for a cruel God, or no God at all.

We may come to relax into and trust the movement of Silence to touch and know itself in the relative world through a gradual process of awakening. We may be assured in knowing that the pure Awareness which permeates everything will awaken itself out of the Dream it has woven itself into. There is no need for that which is unconscious to attempt to willfully effort itself out of unconsciousness. It is for us only to pay attention, listen deeply, and *lean* into our Creator. The limited design detail of the mind's conceptual framework is a part of the functional equation in the overall journey—it is not by any means the master element. The full gamut of humanness *includes* the operational features of the personal self, while rested in the seat of Being. We must be wary of the popular emphasis of "Ego transcendence" and "self-mastery." The clear movement toward the deepest dimension of being is not transcendence of the limited attributes of the personal self, but *surrender by them* to the deepest dimensions of our existence. Of course, that surrender is movement into the unknown.

But imagine what the unknown would be without this nagging sense of a personal self attempting to figure it all out. I suggest that mystery, when it is received without evaluation, is what actually *is*. Look at this directly and you will glimpse the freedom of it. The unknown, seen without the compulsion to *know*, simply reveals what *is* without residue. Then, what *is* ceases to emerge as an unknown,

## The 5th Phenomenon

because the perceiver dissolves into the experience. Ruminate on this point soberly, for it is pointing us to the way out. ✺

# Chapter 17
# The Way Out

I recall the moment leading up to my core surrender clearly to this day. I was sitting on a mud floor, encircled by thick earthen walls—my head hung low. My Ego had reached its capacity to further live out the façade of its conceptual realities. Yet, I was stuck inside my mind and could not find the way out. Such a predicament for me seemed somehow unimaginable. I had dedicated my life to understanding the human condition: I studied all the greatest minds in history; poured over the teachings of every sage philosopher; ruminated on the words of renowned mystics from every corner of the world. I had sat in the presence of living contemporary teachers of consciousness. Liberation, realization, nirvana, sacred unity, illumination, ataraxia, salvation, moksha, awakening, the Tao, redemption, attainment, quantum awareness, cosmic consciousness, enlightenment, ascension—I had studied them all, and understood conceptually that there was a way out of limited consciousness. I even sensed it somewhere other than my mind, in the expansive states I remembered having experienced along the way—but at that moment for me, there was no light of salvation embracing me.

How many people in psych wards, that are on suicide watch, feel the grip of this state of consciousness? How many desperate souls are streaming to mental health practitioners because they are swimming in this condition? How many just sitting in traffic, or even reading this sentence right now? You, who know, or have known this place inside yourself, also might ascertain from reading this book that I have been there. For myself, I recall clearly the maddening wisdom of *no escape*. But from where I stand now, I can tell you that these states of mind are incomplete, and that they do not deserve the credence we so often grant them in those moments of overwhelm. Such psychic wrenching cannot be trusted to contain wisdom because the intellect alone is blind to its own true nature. You must not try to figure out such insanity, or attempt to control the perturbations of it—the whole of you must simply endure the agitations. Endure them because they cannot last. Endure them because they are only an aspect of your existence. Endure those states because that which endures is *larger* than the unrest. But mostly, endure them just because *you can*. I make no promises about bliss waiting for you on the other side of such existential travail, only that there *is* a life beyond it. What actually awaits *you* there, no one can say for sure, but by all means risk *everything* to find out.

But do so only when you are fully willing to take your eyes off the crafted script we all have written for our daily lives. Be open to becoming a fluid, responsive and unpredictable creature that is alive with passion and possibility. When we are sober about this

## The Way Out

commitment, we begin to sense into the tenuous nature of our personality structures—and the rational perspective that rules them. I know that it can feel quite precarious to poke holes in our contrived sense of self through sincere inquiry. Yet, if we are completely dedicated, and can be painfully honest, then one should know that *anything* is possible when in alignment with Presence. To all intrepid souls astride the threshold, be forewarned, the convention of normative social paradigms rarely understands how to embrace those who are living out such a deep consecration to clarity.

While we embark upon the business of confronting our own mechanisms for self-deception, the culture will be quick to tell you that your endeavors for authenticity are problematic; and more than likely go on to diagnose and prescribe the fix for you. Even though the journey may feel isolative at times, we might do well to ask ourselves, for all of the pills, payroll, position or pleasure that society doses out routinely to medicate us, has any of it ever worked to bring an abiding sense of joy, peace, clarity, or true fulfillment to anyone? It seems too obvious to need to mention that coping strategies come from *outside* of us, and therefore rob us of our independent capacity to engage our own inner journey directly. The supply and demand operations of social intercourse are the trappings of an outward enterprise, and have no place in the cultivating of a free and clear consciousness within. What value could there possibly be in using social devices to overlook what is alive inside of us? The ability to feel life deeply is our saving grace. Don't mute it. Don't run from it. Don't deny it. Don't drug it. Don't try and fix it. Let it open you up, because that is the first step out of the existential straightjacket most of humanity finds itself in.

German writer Johann Wolfgang von Goethe's (1749-1832 CE) most famous character, Faust, made a bargain with the devil's servant Mephistopheles. In exchange for his soul, Faust opted for worldly distractions to mitigate the existential burdens of boredom, depression and meaning. Mephistopheles, hinting at the inequity of the agreement, even counsels Faust against the devil's offer, but Faust in the midst of his suffering enters into the contract anyway. We must not make deals with life from the sealed pressure cooker of thought. Even Mephistopheles understood to consider the all-consuming nature of fire, and not just the simmering contents of the pot amid the flames. Such myopic perception invokes error of the most fundamental order.

When I first met my wife, Lenni, she was 25 years old and in the thick of plowing through the intense confusion of the typical human distortions we all confront. She was searching for a way out of the insanity, toward an authentic connection to Life. We often have no idea of the incredible scope of freedom and potential that is dormant inside of us, but Lenni was possessed of a strong sense of it. No one in her peer group at that time seemed to relate to this part of her. Like all genuine seekers, she longed for a deeper order of living more than she wanted to hold on to the fiction most of us typically create around the illusion we take ourselves to be.

Her profound consecration to radical sincerity had brought her to an extreme place of existential crisis in the months just before we met. The power of that experience had opened her in a way that few people let themselves become available to Life. After we met, I witnessed her make difficult strides in conscious evolution rapidly, and capture depths of understanding in her 20s that took me twice as long to realize in my life. Lenni expressed to me that what I had uncovered with AFT was of enormous significance to her. She invited me to consider that what I shared with her also needed to be shared with others. Before I met her, the premise of Awareness Field Theory existed as a file with scattered notes and a flurry of essays partially undertaken. Had she not come along, most likely it would have remained that way.

Once I committed to the project of presenting AFT as *The 5$^{th}$ Phenomenon*, part of the challenge in formulating the book came in recognizing that there are so many different kinds of people moving from qualitatively different places of awareness that would be reading it. I questioned who exactly might benefit from what the material offered. The landscape of varied consciousness in human beings appeared full of stark contrasts. What kind of person would this work appeal to? As I began writing the book the contents hinted at a correlation that revealed some clues.

I conjured an analogy of each individual's human evolutionary potential to a stream with silt, rocks, and boulders in it. I imagined some people to be like fine silt and sand; others more like tumbled rocks; and then there were those who were like massive eight-foot diameter boulders in five-foot deep water. I saw Life itself as the moving current in that river. The evolution of the material in that confluence would be dependent on the aforementioned nature of the substances that occupy it—and people mirrored that dynamic.

"Silt type" people I saw as being swept away by the current—they are often moved, but not shaped by the experience of life. "Boulder-like" people I imagined being mechanically sculpted by the water's flow against their immovable station—thus they are worn over time and molded in predictable fashion. River rock people are sometimes tumbled, and at other times settled within the flow of water—they become modeled by the dynamic experience into something unique and unpredictable. River rocks are always randomly sensual forms, without edge or manufactured symmetry.

So it translates this way: The consciousness of some human beings is intractably lodged into the riverbed of life, and the heavy mass will be worn into an amorphous shape by the consistent flow of current against it (Boulders). Other people appear bereft of the substantive content of their subjective existence, and they are easily swept away, being transported, but not fundamentally changed by this life (Silt). And then there are those who are possessed of such optimum proportion as to be at intervals tumbled from station to station. Being influenced by the fluid flow of life, river stones are neither stuck in one place nor continually suspended in the water's motions. I imagine river rock people as dynamically shaped, not statically worn nor carried away. These types become transformed, not just eroded or floated in solution. We must all eventually ascribe to the way of the *tumbled river rock* if we are to evolve to our fullest potential—or we will be left to endure the phlegmatic existence of silt and boulders. Though modern society cultivates for the boulder and silt lifestyle, this book is for all those who find a good measure of river rock in their souls.

There is so much information out there pressing each of us to be a stable and responsible person, and to do so while operating in an incredibly misguided social environment that emphasizes obedience to a cold productivity. Time and again we are offered methods to *not* feel the current of life at the depth discussed in this book, because the word on the street is to be that open implies weakness, and will only lead to your demise or lack of success in the culture. The pundits pandering to those who covet the promise of numbingly smooth operation inside social paradigms are pervasive. Endless programs promise us health, well-being, and realization of the abundant life through the control or transforming of thoughts and emotions—all designed to sidestep a direct embrace of life through a cunning craft of self-deception. No social product can legitimately promise others a magic carpet ride to a direct experience of existence through the sole administration of systems of practice, or doctrines of belief. Adrenaline or positive thinking will not blast us into a truly genuine and fulfilling life. A strong personal drive focused only on select positive attributes does not represent real courage, nor does it model genuine leadership. The rational prudence that defines cultural deftness is often little more than the product of a fixed and socially indoctrinated life. Evolution by its very nature always disrupts the normative zeitgeist, so the world-shakers of consciousness must inevitably be authors of a novel existence.

There is a way out of this life-depleting labyrinth we have come to call civilization. The massive proselytization of every child into functioning only from thought consciousness nurtures just the *façade* of awareness. We have been misled. Our organic design is so much more complete and larger than what we have been shown. The first step away from a cultured hypnosis is realizing that. Pericles (494-429 BCE), the great Athenian statesman, summed it up best some 2,500 years ago:

## The 5th Phenomenon

> *"Others are brave out of ignorance; and when they begin to think, they begin to fear. But those who can most truly be accounted as brave are they who know the meaning of what is sweet in life—and what is terrible, and then go out undeterred to meet what is to come."*

When you do go out "undeterred to meet what is to come," be assured that for millennia, other brave souls before you have embarked upon their own version of the path to clarity. Know that contemporaries you have never met are engaged in that journey right now. Know too that others will stand on the foundations of your courageous life to find inspiration to do the same in their own way. If all you can do is imagine that kind of bravery right now, then listen to the story of those who have captured it for all time. ✪

# Chapter 18
# Listening

There is an allegory about feeding stray animals that show up on your doorstep—the ones you choose to feed tend to come back. What we pay attention to becomes energized by the very attention we give it. When we understand the import of this, we can see the depth of responsibility associated with it, because whatever we encourage to return back to our doorstep usually wants to come back to stay. When we feed feral thoughts, we must understand that they are looking for a home. The free-floating human psyche is a very needy creature, especially when it is severed from the fields of Source awareness that give rise to it. The fragmented mind that has become unconscious of its true nature is, in effect, an orphan—a motherless child wanting to be taken care of. Our response to that indigent waif must move beyond sentimentality or rejection; we must see with a receptivity that responds from a whole seeing.

This is the reason that we must pay attention to our lives; we must *fully* listen. We must receive all that is available to us as conscious creatures. The entire dimensionality of our existence is relating and interfacing on many levels, and we must retain a receptive posture to all of it. This kind of listening is an essential skillset to the art of living. The quality of attention that fields the full scope of experience we are immersed in however, is no easy task to cultivate. The difficulty arises because we have been taught to limit our perceptions only to the physical senses, and then confine our interpretations about what is happening to our thinking mind only. The isolative landscape of the intellect alone is the foster home where the orphaned sense of self lives out its wasteland creed. We must not sponsor the Ego's coping mechanism of frivolous desire and aversion cycles with nourishing awareness. Instead, we must listen at the very depths of consciousness so that we may respond from Being, expressing only that which is influenced by Presence.

I describe this order of hearing as a non-positioned listening (from all levels of our being) to the full dimensional content of what we are receiving. Comprehensive listening eventually unfolds into a centered and locatable response within the receiver. The receptive movement is expansive, non-linear and absolutely open. There is an assimilation of the whole product that is being experienced. This is not to say that we are in an evaluative posturing. This quality of receptivity is an arrangement of *harmonic curiosity*. Receptive listening has no agenda, any more than the black void of space has a motive to absorb radiation—there is no such pretense. Listening at any given moment, without being connected to the Presence of the Creator however, is like trying to put together a jigsaw puzzle without ever seeing the whole picture first. We become lost in a few related pieces here and there that fit together, but the whole content never actualizes because we aren't seeing that large. Harmonic curiosity invokes a revelation of the full dimensional context of the matter, offering more than just segregated perceptions for the intellect to try and piece together.

Locating response within, after the movement of harmonic curiosity has made contact with another, is the second aspect of true listening. I love the congregational protocol of the Quakers who derive their name from the custom of refraining from speech or any demonstrative acts in church until the spirit has moved them so profoundly that they begin to tremble and "quake" with the truth bursting forth from inside them. I have been to Quaker meetings, and always admired the deep reverence I sensed for this sanctity around listening for the truth, and the silent respect they carried knowing that a compelling revelation might be bestowed upon a "friend" at any time. This is the closest example I can relate when citing my own moment-to-moment experience of finding response from deep listening. Sometimes my sense of genuine response calls for nothing further than remaining in the receptive state without reply. Often the most profound act is being still, but routinely I am moved to *act* from stillness. I am continually excited to discover how Life will choose to respond through me, and I feel a delightful anticipation about what will be revealed to others and myself in these exchanges.

There are two key elements to engaging a full listening posture. The first is *absolute transparency*, and the other is an unmitigated *capacity to feel*. Transparency means an unfiltered openness to the full spectrum of dimensional sentience within oneself and in another. The capacity to fully feel means we do not avoid, shun, shutdown, suppress, ignore, repress or otherwise dismiss how we are personally receiving our experiences. In all my years of studying consciousness there were two bodies of work that stood out as the most powerful tools toward aiding my ability to listen with Presence. Interestingly enough they were not studies in psychology, ontology or spirituality. They were healing modalities that organically necessitated availability to Being.

The initial body of work I encountered that provided a profound shift in awareness—and subsequent deepening into receptivity—was a seemingly simple conflict resolution language model introduced by Dr. Marshall Rosenberg (1934-2015 CE), with whom I studied for four years starting in 1996. The second focus of study was an even more unlikely candidate. The ancient healing work called Jin Shin Jyutsu became a practice in unspoken listening and intuitive awareness, and functioned as an excellent complement to Rosenberg's model. I find it useful to share a little bit about each of these bodies of work, and how they not only taught me the art of listening, but also how they influenced aspects of my formulations around AFT.

Dr. Rosenberg's work is known as Non Violent Communication or NVC. It involves the capacity to both locate and feel the impulses of emotional states within us and then interpret them by navigating the psychologically relevant needs that are driving them. Emerging from a background in Psychology (he carried a Ph.D. in the field), Rosenberg was profoundly affected by the pioneering efforts of psychologist Carl Rogers (1902-1987 CE) and his emphasis on the utilization of empathic rapport for therapeutic effect in mental health patients. Rogers referred to this empathic rapport as an "unconditional positive regard," which Rosenberg often simplified as a "caring connection" to the feelings and needs of others. The genius of Rosenberg was his insistence on the importance of locating the feeling state before moving into any subsequent cognitive considerations. I believe he understood instinctually—beyond Rogers' empathic elucidations—that true healing only begins when we are *feeling* life, and that this was an essential movement before intellectual processing could be of any significant use. Rosenberg was often overheard saying "empathy before education."

To "feel" in AFT, means to allow an experience to penetrate the armor of the psyche, and strike deep into the heart of the receiver in order to discover a whole and organic human response, instead of merely an emotional reaction arising from the personality's psychic structure. To truly *feel* in this way is to build spaciousness around the whole body's response as we interface with the circumstances of life. Once the body's story is revealed, we then maintain the requisite receptivity to that which guides us from the transpersonal awareness realm with knowledge that only the Creator Intelligence would offer. Rosenberg concretized the psychology of this process by distilling out of its essence a simple reduction that shaped a four-step model that formulated what he called the "language of the heart." Rosenberg's ability to capture such nuanced discernment into secular language represents a stroke of brilliance. I believe it has allowed access to deeper awareness of psychic structures by a broad cross-section of people that otherwise might not be moved to engage such rich internal psycho-emotional terrain. I once asked Rosenberg in private if he was aware of what I saw as the radically deconstructive nature of his basic model—how it passively invoked a deep self-intimacy that undid the psyche—and he acknowledged that he clearly understood that. When I further inquired as to why he would not reveal that insight to those who showed interest in his work, he said that he actively avoided acknowledging the profound depth work inherent in the model because he thought, "few would come or commit to the process if they knew." Though I had a deep personal affection for Rosenberg, on this last point I respectfully acknowledged that I could not agree, knowing that my own work necessitated shattering limiting beliefs in human motivation and potential.

Nevertheless, the NVC model still ranks as a profound life-serving contribution. The four-step process invites discrimination between thought and feeling that becomes essential to clarity, because thinking alone has never manifested a complete state of consciousness. Thoughts are static by nature, but feelings are sourced in life-affirming energy that is fluid and not rationally confined. Dr. Rosenberg also advocated discernment between pseudo-feeling perceptions and pure emotion. He taught that only emotion-based feelings point toward a somatic dimension of sentience that is not limited to the narrow reflections of mental cognition where violence is born. He understood better than anyone I had ever met that the rational mind alone objectifies what it sees, and in so doing strips everything of its *living* dimensional essence. His insights grant us a tangible means into accessing a more comprehensive quality of consciousness. The NVC process aids us in cultivating an awareness that is deeper than the mind's incessant narrative. In short, we discover a living current that leads us into the complete heart of life. The ability to navigate our own inner processes and establish for ourselves a transformative posture of receptivity to life, allows us then to also listen deeply to others.

This art of discernment distinctly illuminates the fact that receptivity and genuine listening cannot happen cunningly. Intellectual shrewdness is not only useless toward authentic Presence, it is a distraction and a depletion. Feelings will always lead to the depths of subjective consciousness, the place where we must begin our own work of profound release into life. Once we arrive at the authentic feeling state and experience it fully, we may appeal to intuitive wisdom from impersonal Being for guidance. This is the movement beyond conceptual paradigms that listens deeply enough to marry the very heart of Presence with the direct experience of the body.

A discussion about maintaining a position of transparency to life affirming Presence leads me to the second body of work that profoundly influenced my unfolding—that of the ancient healing work of Jiro Murai's (1886-1960 CE) Jin Shin Jyutsu (JSJ). Within the craft of this physiological art, once we have learned to physically listen to the body (by listening to pulses), we learn to listen to insight. The deep rapport I found with JSJ arose because it cultivated an intuitive quality of listening like no other practice I had come across. Listening with JSJ sidestepped language and offered a quality of connection that was void of the pitfalls of hearing only from concept-based consciousness. The process reminded me of Helen Keller's (1880-1968 CE) 1903 autobiography *The Story of My Life*. In it she cites how as a blind and deaf child she initially received and experienced life through a state of consciousness that was void of any and all concepts. The quality of her apprehension before learning language came out of *pure awareness receptivity*.

JSJ facilitated a more dimensionally rich connection to others by inviting me to stop thinking, and begin *sensing* to the full presentation of life in another person's body. "Jin Shin Jyutsu" roughly translates from the original Japanese as "The Art of The Creator as Practiced Through Human Beings." The JSJ teaching regarding the detailed design and function of the human body is ancient, dating back to the first Vedic Rishis of India. Beyond listening to the pulses of the body's meridians (much like acupuncture), it involves a dimensional aspect of receptivity that elevates the somatic practice to an artistic endeavor. In addition to the observation of the physical manifestations of disharmony within the body, there is also the holding of one's attention to make room for the intuitive illumination of the practitioner by Presence. Since the healing practice is held as a reverential application of Creator design wisdom, the consciousness around the actual hands-on work includes an active attenuation to the Intelligence that authors the systems we are immersed in. This transparency taught me to listen with all the appropriate intention and humble openness required to receive the wisdom needed in the moment to affect harmonization of the body of the receiver during JSJ sessions. I have come to realize that so much of my work involved, and involves to this day, *listening*.

Through JSJ, I learned the art of being receptive to the full dimension of another's body, while simultaneously being attenuated to my own intuition and insight—both of which symbiotically informed me of the present moment, of the person I was engaged with, and the nature of our relationship. Through NVC, I learned how to listen to verbalized conceptual representations and find the fluid life energy they were pointing to. Through extensive practice of both fields of work I found there was a distinct discernment between what I term *willful listening* and the deeper movement of *receptive sensing*.

Willful listening, I determined, was simply the applied intellectual review of another's expressions. The posture (common to mental health diagnosticians) is cold and evaluative, and it feels that way to the one who is sharing or being examined. Receptive listening, on the other hand, elicits surrender in the heart of the receiver as one takes in the experience of the expresser. The whole being listens to the whole being of another. This movement is not about an intellectual acuity, or even emotional deftness. Instead, it is the co-mingling of clear and authentic Presence without an evaluative subjective posturing. To know the art of clear receptivity is to know the craft of true listening. To be touched by Life in this way, by letting the full dimensional experience of listening entirely move through oneself without the subjective mind commandeering the moment, is high art. This practice of sacred rapport is the essential skill upon which all of life's relational finesse should be predicated. In this profound context, true vulnerability is not weakness; it is the capacity to feel and sense fully, without guard or filter. But the art does take practice.

Many individuals find it difficult to grasp the craft of not *trying* to be present and listen. In such circumstances the mind tries to get involved yet again, running down methods and programs to "locate" serenity within, while manifesting its *version* of being fully available to hear another. This is a fundamental hurdle for so many people that are sincerely seeking profound clarity. The mind always looks to execute what it perceives of as the meaningful *task* of tranquil presence, by overriding the requisite sensing and feeling into life that would elicit it. The dynamic expresses itself in the common colloquialism of *overthinking*.

This is why meditation or prayer geared toward stilling the body-mind, or making it "one-pointed," or even redirecting thought toward a desired utility, always seemed off-point and incomplete to me. The sought-after enlightenment in instances of prayer or meditation—in my experience—became just another conceptual plan enjoined to spiritually colored supplications. Meditative invocation seemed ironically saturated with structure and expectation. The imposition of regimes of sitting still while suppressing, imposing, or otherwise willfully managing thoughts and feelings was for me worse than unproductive—I actually found it to be a source of insult to my body. In all my years of exploring such methods, the practices never led to anything fruitful, no matter who the teacher was, or what doctrine they arose out of.

Actual breakthroughs in touching stillness in my case would come from explorations of life-enriching work like NVC and JSJ — not from the prescribed serenity of spiritual environments or practices. The posture of service suited me much better than did any intention-based spiritual or religious practices whose functions seemed cumbersomely focused on "me" as the meditator/prayer. By sharing my personal processes, I do not intend to declare the folly of other paths or approaches—or to even emphasize my own as superior. It's just that I find it significant that during my "seeking" years, spiritual teachers placed so much emphasis on some form of practice to "awaken," never once offering the notion that my *personal passions* might serve to be the most effective path to deepening my experience with Presence. So I have come to encourage everyone to consider the value in finding their own way by becoming intimate with their particular talents and interests. Our individual gifts and endowments hold the key to so much wisdom, because I feel those insights would be uniquely tailored to the individuals they are bestowed upon. The aboriginal peoples of the Americas appropriately called these personal path features an individual's *medicine*.

Listening has always felt like a sacred act to me. Both NVC and JSJ allowed me to learn how to listen artfully and with poignant clarity, all while being in some posture of active *service to another*. Certainly, over the course of my journey I did devote significant amounts of time contemplating my existence by studying those who had done the same, but those instances were more occasions of my personal curiosity seeking something. Those activities did not *directly* yield shifts in consciousness. I was, in fact, never compelled through any program designed to invoke spiritual evolution or attainment, to achieve anything more than incidental insights. But my work as a practitioner of JSJ and NVC contributed richly to my life by transforming my consciousness, making it much more fluid than it was in my earlier years.

The many skillsets I have learned and integrated allow me to be free to respond to the Intelligence of the Creator itself as it permeates every moment through my instrument. When listening to Presence, I no longer feed the "orphan" of isolated thought by virtue of some unconscious default. My subjective consciousness has finally married that which gifted me the faculty of awareness itself, preparing me to give and receive a new order of transmission. ✪

# Chapter 19
## Transmission

Stillness of Being is the Source of all individuated consciousness features. This is the meaning of the saying attributed to Jesus, "When two or more are gathered in my name, there I am in their midst." What Christ refers to as "I am," is simply Creator Presence manifesting as still and undifferentiated awareness prior to individual consciousness. Since the ubiquitous stillness of Creator Presence is unified, absolute and unalterable, it is only the specific sentience attributes themselves that come under the influence of relational rapport. Pure awareness is the unaffected solution within which the experiencer, like a particle, is suspended. Varying states of transmission that occur as a product of interpersonal communion visit only upon the subjects involved—the essence of pure awareness abides untouched.

When human beings undertake interpersonal exchange, the overall source and content of the "give and take" is not limited to the intellect or even to the bodies themselves. There is also a transaction of awareness field content. This relationship is more profound than any of the more tangible aspects of interaction typically associated with interpersonal communication. When subjective consciousness comes under the influence of the directed sentience of another, both the expressive *and* receptive agent's tonal posture of consciousness define the quality of rapport—and the net result. The interaction is always predicated on the quality of alchemy that arises between the two (or more) entities whose awareness fields have intersected. AFT delineates the effect of the exchange on the recipient as *transmission*.

Utilizing AFT with people over the decades, I have observed that actual transmission between two individuals can appear to be "zero sum" if only one person in the relational exchange is not fully listening or being consciously present. Even the most potent and passionately offered vibrations can land on barren soil and produce no signs of effective transmission. Conversely, those who are completely conscious and present can extract profound content as a receiver from the most unconscious human expressions. Transmission takes two forms within AFT models. The first I refer to as *transient transmission*, and the second I refer to as *transformative transmission*.

Transient transmission occurs when the individual listening is not fully present and available. Distracted receivers tend to only capture partial aspects because the quality of their attention is itself fragmented. Those possessing a condition of divided consciousness experience the act of reception as limited primarily to conceptual integration, because deeper resonations from the message have become compromised by the listener's splintered receptive posture. Apprehension under these circumstances tends to lack acquisition of the full scope of wisdom that might be available from the content that is being communicated. This is why rapport at this level of exchange is not fundamentally transformative. Interestingly enough, transient transmission has been accepted as normative for most relational interactions.

Transformative transmission is of a whole other order. During transformative transmission, the receiver is in alignment with full Presence while undertaking the act of relational exchange. Transmission in this case becomes transformative at every level of subjective being, from DNA to psychology. The profound shift occurs because there is an alchemical modifier arising out of the uninhibited awareness field rapport between interacting subjects. That factor is also prompting a permanent evolution of the individuals involved. The actual conceptual content of the expresser in this case is of incidental usefulness after the transformative effect has been realized because the relational exchange is predicated on conscious evolution and not content acquisition. This is how human ritual prompts transformative experiences. Such transformation is immediate and intimate, and to a fundamental degree the dynamic knows no real limitation. When parties in clarity are in relational rapport of this nature, the participants are no longer the same people after the exchange—even if the exchange is cursory. There is a profound significance to transformative transmission because every person that learns this craft of exchange contributes to the overall shift of the human condition toward coherency.

Barring the cultivated ability on the part of the receiver to manifest full presence within relational exchange, there are key personal values through which transformative transmission can still occur for the relative neophyte. Those aspects are manifested through the distinctly human virtues of *curiosity*, *love*, and *integrity*. These are the ideal qualities for those in a student or disciple role to utilize until they can manifest clear and mature receptivity from depth consciousness without guidance. The three aforementioned characteristics allow transmission to become transformative to the receiver even when conscious perception is unripe, or languishing in the divergent state. A listener's qualities of devotion, trust and sincerity rendered to a genuine teacher or guiding influence, can override the posture of disjoined consciousness within the learner. Applying these characteristic features allows for the deeper transmission to become transformative enough to penetrate the student's unripe sentience. It is worthwhile to touch into the qualities of each of these virtues from an AFT perspective.

*Curiosity* is a powerful, receptive virtue that is available to all human beings. The posture of curiosity suggests an open state of invitation to clarity and transformation. Learning from a condition of genuine curiosity is not mitigated by an individual's lack of conscious maturity. Children and animals are prime examples of immature or unsophisticated consciousness, respectively, yet they are both masters of being receptive to transformative transmission through learning that is engaged with pristine curiosity.

*Integrity* is another portal to receiving transformative transmission. Integrity can always leverage deep reception from the sophomore consciousness, if the integrity is passionate enough. Deep authenticity can quiet scattered consciousness and make it available to transformative essence. Intermittent windows of clarity and receptivity are often the hallmark of unfolding consciousness in its budding stages, and the powerful keynote of integrity can pull the committed listener through the awkwardly oscillating stages of instability that can arise when we are still learning. Integrity brings an irrational emphasis to being genuine at all costs. This virtue figured prominently in my own process.

*Love* is the most potent virtue available to directly access transformation. Love is boundless, unrestrained and unmitigated possibility. Ardent tenderness directed outward always induces transformative transmission, and it also courts a transformational response from the self when directed inward. Pure love is powerful, cutting through any and all psychic distortions instantly, finding the heart of the intended recipient, and suffering no diminishment in potency from the journey. Love can even penetrate the damaged fabric of the body's various physical and mental debilitations, effecting direct and profound transformation where and when nothing else can reach.

The personal virtues of *pure love*, *sterling integrity*, and *profound curiosity* travel the ethereal highways of human consciousness, and like a substance in solution they abide always suspended in our field of awareness. Through them, transformational transmission becomes the doorway to an evolution of being. Until we are whole, and our consciousness rests in routine clarity, these precious human virtues can work to mend the fractures and fissures in our psychic walls.

As profound and valuable as transmission is, seen in its proper context, it merely unfolds new horizons of dimensionality within the overall evolution of consciousness. The next movement invites us to what I consider the ultimate act of human expression—that of pure surrender to Creator Presence. Christ approaches the *threshold* of this great renunciation in the wilderness. Jesus' dance with the devil in the desert transforms his mortal vessel so that for him, the movement into total clarity becomes algorithmically irrevocable. The soul that emerges from the wilderness of temptation has crossed the threshold of profound choice and ascended into the sublime Presence of "no choice." The Jesus that once dreamed of personal free will is now fully occupied by the Christ that moves solely from the eternal Presence that evaporates volition. The act of deep and passionate *listening* has brought about a radical transfiguration, which in the end allows for the final redemptive gesture of full surrender on the cross to be realized. ✪

# Chapter 20
# Surrender

How does one soul speak to another about surrender? Each person's contract with Life is so incredibly intimate. With our body we straddle that exquisite razor's edge where one lung respires on the subtle domain of mysterious essence, and the other inhales the thick ethers of this physical world. We cannot choose one and leave the other, for always, two lungs serve one heart. We may be born into separation, but we are designed to exist whole, through the surrender of all.

As we engage each moment, there arises in conjunction with our sensing of impersonal awareness fields, also the total content of our mortal humanness. True surrender has never fundamentally been about "letting go" of anything temporal because actual surrender is a flow, a movement comprising the *full* dimensional substance of our existence. Surrender is not a particular act, perpetrated by a singular individual, defined by certain intent, emphasizing a precise conclusion. The leading edge of a flash flood finds its way over arid terrain not by disassociating itself from the volume of water feeding it, but by feeling the *surging influence of the whole* mass as it moves. Water presses out across those landscapes not only by virtue of the hydraulic push from behind, but also by the countless variables that are present at its leading edge. This is similar to seamless surrender within human consciousness. We feel and sense all, moving organically and spontaneously, yet without definitive volition. The whole movement of surrender is too sublime to be scripted, and if we are unripe or lack the requisite wisdom, the psyche will often recoil in the presence of such subtle deliberations because the mind's nature seeks control by default.

There is a contraction, a tension in the body that knows what it is to *control*. That holding is born of fear. From the moment we emerge from the womb, the genetically hardwired instinct to survive grips us. We writhe, open our eyes, and as all creatures have done before us, press into life and begin the struggle to exist. But there is a distinct difference between surviving and *thriving*. Animals are meant to survive, but humans are designed to *live*. That means that our response to life carries with it a deeper measure of dimension than simply perpetuating our physical existence—our unique design as creatures offers something more.

At some point an absolute circumstance arrives that we cannot control—at physical death we return to Silence. In that very instance, no matter what our outlook or disposition, we *will* let go. Surrender will be the texture of your last breath when that time comes. What will be the quality of your respiration in that hour? It will be much like the millions before it. Cultivate surrender into your respiration while you live, and you will be gifted the peaceful feel of it in your last exhale when you die.

Animals have a natural relationship with surrender; at death they release far better than most humans. That is because they have not lived a lifetime of psychic distortion that sets itself apart from nature. Animals struggle to survive, yes, but always under the organic endowment of grace, and amid the ordered operations of the Tao. Animals can move from fear or ferocity to relative calm and contentedness without moving through the stations of resistance that bind humans to the cold steel of the psychic structure's volatility. Animals are not bitter, they do not foment, nor do they cling or regret.

Conscious surrender for humans becomes an *ongoing meditation* into the seamless receptivity of Being; it is a marriage of the timeless attention within us to the eternal Presence of the Creator. With this art there is no internal effort or existential struggle because the sublime enrichment of Creator Intelligence defines every action in our lives when we are attenuated to it. In *Prometheus Unbound*, poet Percy Bysshe Shelley (1792-1882 CE) puts it this way:

> *The loathsome mask has fallen, the man remains*
> *Scepterless, free, uncircumscribed, but man*
> *Equal, unclassed, tribeless, and nationless,*
> *Exempt from awe, worship, degree, the king*
> *Over himself…*
> *And women too, frank, beautiful and kind…*
> *From custom's evil taint exempt and pure;*
> *Speaking the wisdom once they could not think,*
> *Looking emotions once they feared to feel*

> *And changed to all which once they dared to be,*
> *Yet being now, made earth like heaven.*

Ultimately, the keynote of successful surrender can only follow an absolute extraction of the tenacious root of narcissism from the seat of consciousness. Yet surrender is a doorway that is opened from the inside, not an entrance that is battered down from outside by an Ego armed with a search warrant and looking for enlightenment. Surrender is a process that is not delivered on our terms, because it is not fundamentally a personal accomplishment. True existential release manifests as a *response* to an invitation from Life itself. Our reply to this offer becomes an active acceptance and reception of grace—the movement is sublime, and not fraught with the dramatic import often associated with it. To be certain, surrender flows—it has no foundation. The journey of surrendering continues unfolding until the critical equation culminates into the sublime release of absolute *deliverance*, which itself can never be construed as an arrival.

Jesus announces from the cross, "It is finished," and one is compelled to deliberate what this last known utterance actually means. To be certain, Jesus' final acts on this earth display a culmination of Presence that knows no insulation from the complex labyrinth of the human psyche. Nor is he sheltered from the massive cross-projections that occur as a function of his intimate interactions with others. All is absorbed and redeemed through Jesus by the immutable Presence of Being. This makes Christ the quintessential heroic figure—his life has come full circle having thoroughly navigated all points of existence—and from the cross he is delivered back to Source, pellucid and complete.

The depth of surrender that Jesus achieves under crucifixion breaches an unprecedented and absolute threshold within the human condition—one that has never been approached through the practice of even the most austere and inspired contemplations. The achievement moves deeper than the clarity of the Tao, is more profound than scripture or sutra wisdoms—realizing potential that surpasses even the pristine state of enlightenment. Christ's mystical surrender plunges humanity immediately into apotheosis, ushering in a new era that heralds the actualization of our *complete* potential. Through Jesus' passionate transmutation, the author of creation has now consciously touched itself in human form, in complete freedom, and without subjective contraction. Through Jesus' redemptive journey, the Alpha and Omega of existence has been realized, and the unfolding for the rest of human kind continues. AFT is affirming, two thousand years later, that pure release into the absolute clarity of consciousness has now become the manifested birthright of our species.

The epic surrender of Jesus naturalizes transparency of the body to luminous Presence—establishing supreme intimacy with impersonal Being. For Christ, all psychic constructs have not only been redeemed, they have been burned to the ground by the fires of an eternal surrender. "It is finished." Jesus now stands amid the world of concept and reason as if it were a wasteland of ash, and sees that only Noumenal Awareness remains—and to *that* Presence all existence is forever wed. ✽

# CHAPTER 21
# We the People

How often do we witness rampant corruption in the seats of social power? It seems that no matter where we look, organizations appear rife with greed, violence and oppression of some sort and degree. Government, religion, business, gangs, cartels, mafias, militants and assorted other special interest groups vie for power, influence, and control daily. It is an overwhelming task just to keep track of all the manifold regimes, let alone try and confront the whole of them to effect fundamental changes. AFT offers another possibility.

The trajectory of the above viewpoint could be predicated on the assumption that there is a villain—some person or some group of people, who are responsible for the plethora of social injustices. In military terms, locating and eradicating the "hard target" eliminates the problem. Yet the systems involved in social corruption do not conform to such tidy strategies, because the challenges we face are not sourced from any exact point of venality. It may seem counter-intuitive, but from an AFT perspective the actual problem lies with the oppressed majority and not so much with the minority of regime despots disseminating tyranny. I offer that the target of reform lies not with the miscreant heads of social power, but directly at the seat of the subjugated. Those that are abusing the station of socio-cultural control hope that we, as a world population, never come to this realization.

They are depending on the whole of humanity to remain distracted and preoccupied with the "evil-doer," because they know that the systems they have created are impervious to any real internal reformation, a crafted detail that insulates and solidifies their construct of ruling power. As long as the oppressed remain believing that the enemy is confined to the few in power, the focus remains on "storming the castle" where the malefactors are ensconced. The usual cost of storming the castle, however, will remind the revolutionaries that resistance is too costly, or even futile, and they will again be relegated to a servile despair. Even if the revolt finds success, the reformation that follows often becomes seeded in the same system soil that the former oppressor occupied, and the new fruit eventually bears another form of spoiled produce—no matter how noble the revolution.

The day that *mass* consciousness begins to realize that the impenetrable fortress of social power becomes a crypt without the support and participation of the people is the day that the tyrants come down from the tower and crawl across the drawbridge in humble supplication. No seat of power is perpetuated without mass confirmation, submission and servitude. There is no way to deny the indirect yet brazen accountability we all have for aiding and abetting corrupt systems, simply by virtue of our flourishing within them. I imagine that at some point, the future of humanity will look back at their ancestors in wonder at how so many that were decent, followed the few that were nefarious, for so long. Yet what were our unconscious ancestors to do *without* the instrument of force? Confrontational insurrection of unprincipled regimes combined with a vision for reform was their standard for revolution. Anarchy employs insurrection without order, but only foments destructive chaos—because anarchy is simply rebellion without vision. Those old standards of change are becoming defunct, because we require evolution for the new age.

In the new light, the imminent subject of change becomes the individual that desires the change. One by one, we make up—and wake up—the whole. The majority cannot reform a debased minority without the power of massive solidarity. But authentic cohesive unity cannot arise without each of us expressing an individual coherency of consciousness that is attenuated to clarity. And finally, we must recognize that clarity itself cannot continue to be unalloyed when it becomes something that is positioning itself for control, or even victory. We must recognize that the healthiest culture arises organically from a radically free environment. This is the *real* revolution.

Ultimately, we must learn not to be drawn into the dramas of distortion while obsessing over the vice that comprises them, because the ensuing reactivity perpetuates more degeneration—not the requisite enrichment from Being that can truly transform systems of tyranny. Communist revolutionary V.I. Lenin (1870-1924 CE) discovered, when he descended upon Russia's 1917 post-Czar power vacuum, that high-minded ideals are not enough. In the absence of an enlightened people to govern, the governor must inevitably become the brutal dictator of absolute power. The system of communist doctrine, in theory, was supposed to eventually make all central authority obsolete. That idealism mutated in short order into the statistically most vicious militaristic regime in history—and one that finally collapsed under its own heartless weight. Throughout the ages, the notion of benevolent rule has in fact never amounted to much more than a façade—a political platform that attempts to mask authoritarian rule but is destined to *control* unconscious masses.

The revolution that brings about evolution can only arise with the deliberate considerations of depth consciousness—a dimension that recognizes the *whole* human condition. This process requires patience, courage, and unwavering commitment to the wisdom that points to something larger than our "selves" as individuals. This incarnation of revolution is different than armed rebellion, which has had its place and time in history. The nature of creating change by shifting consciousness is of another order. It brings about permanent transformation of our social fabric, not just temporary usurpation that swaps one totalitarian regime for another. This design of revolution starts with individual accountability first—a movement that fosters genuine transformation from within. It progresses one by one, and not with the hype of conceptual propaganda doled out to the masses by overseers of regulation and control.

There is an intimacy and empowerment to such a movement that both requires and solicits a new order of responsibility from the individual. To strive for and achieve clarity of consciousness requires nothing from the world, and so we may begin now, in this very moment. Engaging this artful practice depends upon only one thing—an individual's sincere commitment to do so. This realization in itself is a radical insight. The choice we have to change ourselves, and by extension the world, is the most profound revolution available. We need not concern ourselves with how the larger revolution will unfold "out there." Those conclusions take care of themselves when we take care of our internal revolution first. The magic is never in the wave of the wand; the actual magic occurs when the audience co-creates a shared reality with the magician.

The revolution is at hand, whether we see it or not. The powers that be certainly have no idea what is coming. The new evolution in consciousness cannot be prepared for by offices that would wish to circumvent it, because the dead cannot outflank the living— and you and I *are* the living. We move out of the authentic edge of our own originality, and if each of us individually rejects repeating history, then collectively, we make new waves in the present as the emerging *world* community. We may quietly demonstrate it in our lives without fanfare while the global swell of clear awareness is accumulating velocity. The quiet coalition is shifting the balance of mass consciousness, and at some point the larger transmutation will begin to unfold. French scholar Ernest Renan (1823-1892 CE) put it this way: "...consciousness gives proof of its strength by the sacrifices which demand the abdication of the individual to the advantage of the whole...a present consent that demonstrates the will to live together." For Renan this statement was the definition of a nation, but for AFT it qualifies as the creed of an evolved human consciousness without borders.

Where we will end up is as much a vision as it is a mystery, but one thing is certain: We will not continue to avoid the most obvious attribute in existence (consciousness), and regard it as something not worthy of sincere consideration and genuine inquiry. We can now wisely place it within the pantheon of legitimate phenomena and begin the art of living in accord with the wellspring of insight to which Awareness Field Theory is pointing. The time has certainly arrived for an organic arising of activation toward a clarity of consciousness that is not tethered to the intellectual paradigms of men; a movement that is spontaneous, natural, and free of agenda. The age of concept-chained knowledge has passed, and the age of Creator-infused wisdom, which we derive from the interfacing of a radically dimensional awareness, is upon us.

We can no longer depend solely on academic organizations of thought to liberate and evolve us. They grudgingly accept the magic of mystery, but never acknowledge the magician. They drink from the river, but do not look to discover its source. They directly experience the phenomenon of consciousness and completely overlook its fundamental nature and significance. The scholar will typically fall short because the leash of rationality only extends so far into life—they only dig as deep as mere thought can allow. There is certainly no need to condemn the current limitations of academics, but neither is there a need to invest so much credence in their work as to impose a filter against the whole wisdom of Creator Presence that is available to us.

Belief, too, has had its day. Myth and superstition likely began with primitive man summoning wild stories around the fire, or cave paintings that attempted to give some meaning to the wonders and terrors that those bands of intrepid creatures endured. Those compelling fables developed over time into epic rumors that became legend. Such assembled myth eventually became codified into doctrines of divinity—scriptures that have for too long spoken for us. For centuries they have acted as meddling distant relatives, telling us what to think, what to eat, what to wear, and how to live our lives. The following of such static doctrine may have had its appeal for our ancestors, but the times have changed, *and* are evolving fast. We are at last ready to begin assuming the mantle of responsible self-inquiry into life. We have arrived at the dawning of a new generation that desires to be free of borders, free of ethnicity, free of politics, free of religious dogma, free of provincial culture, free of pundits, and free even of the limiting indoctrinations of formal education. As we become less afraid of the unknown, we become more available to learning what mystery has to reveal.

If our inquiry is sincere, we will find that we are neither alone, nor isolated in our commitment to the inner life. We will seek outwardly only after we have authentically looked within. And when we do look out, we will recognize our resonant world community, quietly embrace it without declaration or spectacle, and begin our work. The true strength and wisdom we acquire will not have been from the world of men, but from the builder of worlds itself. We will not become the disengaged and tired generations that have burned out, or faded away in the past. We come not as an army with banners and weapons, but as unaffiliated individuals with *Presence*;

too many to dismiss, and in numbers great enough to finally shift world consciousness without firing a shot.

I am no prophet, and I do not need to be one to announce and declare that the radical paradigm shift in consciousness is unfolding. It has been quietly growing for some time. Dutch philosopher Benedict de Spinoza (1632-1677 CE) erupted out of the 17th century to proclaim, "The highest virtue lay in restraint guided by a full understanding of the world, and of self." Human beings engaging the art of consciousness of the kind discussed in Awareness Field Theory have already begun to operate out of the clarity that gave rise to Spinoza's anachronistic Renaissance wisdom. Consciousness today is capable of moving in direct association with the Intelligence of the Creator, and restraint from the distortion of fragmented sentience is apprising and shaping our actions.

This is no future prediction. *The 5th Phenomenon* announces what is already alive, declaring that we are in ever-increasing numbers, and exponentially growing every day. No government, no corporation, no religion can stop it; no power on earth can prevent it. We have all suffered long enough, and the time is at hand to shift out of the old ways. May it be known that this new clarity of consciousness is not here to claim or destroy the power-centers of civilization; it is simply, and profoundly, here to respond to Life—a much larger covenant. The order of that response is—and will remain—a mystery, until it unfolds all its revelations. The first principle of Chinese philosopher Sun Tzu's (540-470 BCE) *The Art of War* is "know your enemy," but the old power paradigms of earth cannot predict the nature of the new unfolding, and so they can never confront the authority of mystery. As such, there will be no war against it. There need not be one.

Power paradigms have always been the awkward substitute for true freedom, and true freedom is the birthright of every human being. Even the heavy-laden benefactors of worldly conquest would desire this new order of freedom and beauty if only they understood that it is available—if only they *knew* it was possible for them too. They will eventually learn by example, from ever-increasing numbers, until even the glacial corruption inside them melts into the free-flowing bodies of water they were meant to be. There is no need for indoctrination into true freedom; eventually all will become aware of it through a perpetual and irresistible life transmission. That milestone will be achieved from a momentum established in the velocity of the human heart, as it manifests the compelling beauty of the Creator with clarity, and with passion—one person at a time. This phenomenon is evolving the course of human history without volition, and the best is most certainly yet to come.

The human experience looks so very different to me now than it did to me as a child. I see it expressing itself in ways too incredible to calculate, and too inspired to settle for the old reasonable hopes of our ancestors. The Intelligence to which we have access is operating outside of all definition, and we are married to it. This odd veil of contrived separation from the very Presence that created us is threadbare. It will soon fall completely away. We will finally be fully transparent to the living Presence that touches all things, and what we shall accomplish dwarfs even the grandest of utopic dreams. We will draw seamless inspiration from transcendence itself, and move effortlessly in ways that today would be deemed miraculous or even impossible.

One thing I know is true: The magnificent, unreasonable life awaits. As you come to dance on the edge of that fire, be sure to bring your heart to the occasion. It's okay if you don't know all the answers, just begin with a great question—one that strikes deep, and maybe even seems impossible to reconcile. One like the inquiry my first teacher Alice spoke of: *What is this subtle pretext of purely mortal error?* Let the medicine particular to your own query humble you, while you let its answer open you.

We have been told in so many ways that we are small, powerless and insignificant; that our lives are of little or no consequence. Do not believe this deception. No one tells a drop of water inside a tsunami that it is miniscule and irrelevant. We know the secret and power of moving from the whole.

Do not play small with the grand gift of life. Honor your existence, for the very maker of the cosmos moves inside you without constraint. All sense of limitation is merely a by-product of fractured reason. Discard it.

Move from Presence, and never doubt. It is always the quality of your consciousness, and not the act, which carries and defines the moment.

What created you cannot be severed from you. Do not disenfranchise the soul. *You* affect creation as much as it affects you.

Above all, find your way *home* without dismay my brothers and sisters. Let us all gather round the table that is set there—and never again forget where we come from.

Live your radiance. The light of a single soul is greater than all the darkness of mankind combined.

I am with you. ✡

# AFTERWORD:
# "The Reply"

In *The 5th Phenomenon* I have deliberately attempted to avoid religious and spiritual trappings, and instead present a straightforward approach to consciousness and the art of living out of true clarity. Yet at the same time I have always been curious about those historical figures that achieved a spiritually mythological status. Does the legend surrounding their lives, which ultimately led to *others* creating ecclesiastical doctrines on how to live, hint that these were indeed human beings who had mastered the art alluded to in *The 5th Phenomenon*?

I have always felt that the life of the individual we have come to know as Jesus, if legitimately historical, has not only been misunderstood, but more than likely quite misrepresented. As a child I felt an intimate affinity with this legendary figure, which throughout my youth would often appear in my dreams. What did this person called Jesus actually do and say all those years ago when he lived? And what would this person do and say today?

# The 5th Phenomenon

In 1880 Fyodor Dostoyevsky published *The Brothers Karamazov*, and he died four months later. Chapter 5 of that book is entitled: "The Grand Inquisitor." In it, the Roman Catholic high prosecutor of 16th century Spain discovers Christ has returned, and he is working miracles in the streets of Seville during the height of the Inquisition. The bitter Papal agent has Jesus immediately arrested and thrown in prison. There, the raging old Cardinal engages Christ in an epic challenge to explain and justify himself before the Holy See.

I love the extensive passage of dialogue the old Cardinal unleashes on Jesus in this chapter of the book. It is a wrenchingly hostile dissertation, becoming in its climax a sweeping dismissal of Jesus' ministerial authority. In the end, Jesus says nothing in reply, only answering with a kiss—a beautiful understated touch. Yet I have always wondered what Jesus *would have said* in response, if he had spoken in that imaginary moment.

As a lyrical summary for this book, I decided to author a response that I imagine might have proceeded from a radically clear and passionately human version of Jesus. The dialectic I present functions as an interpretive addendum to much of what I have detailed in this book. It is exciting to discover this Christ-like figure, speaking truth to power in this imagined circumstance that Dostoyevsky depicted over a century ago, because in my heart I see Christ as having moved from an unrivaled depth of consciousness in the world. So in homage to a great Russian writer's last work, I offer first his original chapter, and then my version of a subsequent "Reply" by Christ to the Inquisitor.

# Afterword: "The Reply"

## The Grand Inquisitor
*By F.M. Dostoyevsky*

. . . My poem is set in Spain, at the most dreadful period of the Inquisition, when bonfires glowed throughout the land every day to the glory of God, and in resplendent *autos-da-fe* burned the wicked heretics.

*"Is it Thou? Thou?"*

*But receiving no answer, he adds at once. "Don't answer, be silent. What canst Thou say, indeed? I know too well what Thou wouldst say. And Thou hast no right to add anything to what Thou hadst said of old. Why, then, art Thou come to hinder us? For Thou hast come to hinder us, and Thou knowest that. But dost thou know what will be tomorrow? I know not who Thou art and care not to know whether it is Thou or only a semblance of Him, but tomorrow I shall condemn Thee and burn Thee at the stake as the worst of heretics. And the very people who have today kissed Thy feet, tomorrow at the faintest sign from me will rush to heap up the embers of Thy fire. Knowest Thou that? Yes, maybe Thou knowest it,' he added with thoughtful penetration, never for a moment taking his eyes off the Prisoner. Hast Thou the right to reveal to us one of the mysteries of that world from which Thou hast come?' 'No, Thou hast not; that Thou mayest not add to what has been said of old, and mayest not take from men the freedom which Thou didst exalt when Thou wast on earth. Whatsoever Thou revealest anew will encroach on men's freedom of faith; for it will be manifest as a miracle, and the freedom of their faith was dearer to Thee than anything in those days fifteen hundred years ago. Didst Thou not often say then, "I will make you free"? But now Thou hast seen these "free" men. Yes, we've paid dearly for it, but at last we have completed that work in Thy name. For fifteen* centuries we have been wrestling with Thy freedom, but now it is ended and over for good. Dost Thou not believe that it's over for good?

Thou lookest meekly at me and deignest not even to be wroth with me. But let me tell Thee that now, today, people are more persuaded than ever that they have perfect freedom, yet they have brought their freedom to us and laid it humbly at our feet. But that has been our doing. Was this what Thou didst? Was this Thy freedom? For now for the first time it has become possible to think of the happiness of men. Man was created a rebel; and how can rebels be happy? Thou wast warned, 'Thou hast had no lack of admonitions and warnings, but Thou didst not listen to those warnings; Thou didst reject the only way by which men might be made happy. But, fortunately, departing Thou didst hand on the work to us. Thou hast promised, Thou hast established by Thy word, Thou hast given to us the right to bind and to unbind, and now, of course, Thou canst not think of taking it away. Why, then, hast Thou come to hinder us?'"

The wise and dread spirit, the spirit of self-destruction and non-existence, talked with Thee in the wilderness, and we are told in the books that he "tempted" Thee. Is that so? And could anything truer be said than what he revealed to Thee in three questions and what Thou didst reject, and what in the books is called "the temptation"? And yet if there has ever been on earth a real stupendous miracle, it took place on that day, on the day of the three temptations. The statement of those three questions was itself the miracle. If it were possible to imagine simply for the sake of argument that those three questions of the dread spirit had perished utterly from the books, and that we had to restore them and to invent them anew, and to do so had gathered together all the wise men of the earth- rulers, chief priests, learned men, philosophers, poets- and had

## Afterword: "The Reply"

*set them the task to invent three questions, such as would not only fit the occasion, but express in three words, three human phrases, the whole future history of the world and of humanity- dost Thou believe that all the wisdom of the earth united could have invented anything in depth and force equal to the three questions which were actually put to Thee then by the wise and mighty spirit in the wilderness? From those questions alone, from the miracle of their statement, we can see that we have here to do not with the fleeting human intelligence, but with the absolute and eternal. For in those three questions the whole subsequent history of mankind is, as it were, brought together into one whole, and foretold, and in them are united all the unsolved historical contradictions of human nature. At the time it could not be so clear, since the future was unknown; but now that fifteen hundred years have passed, we see that everything in those three questions was so justly divined and foretold, and has been so truly fulfilled, that nothing can be added to them or taken from them.*

*Judge Thyself who was right—Thou or he who questioned Thee then? Remember the first question; its meaning, in other words, was this: "Thou wouldst go into the world, and art going with empty hands, with some promise of freedom which men in their simplicity and their natural unruliness cannot even understand, which they fear and dread- for nothing has ever been more insupportable for a man and a human society than freedom. But seest Thou these stones in this parched and barren wilderness? Turn them into bread, and mankind will run after Thee like a flock of sheep, grateful and obedient, though for ever trembling, lest Thou withdraw Thy hand and deny them Thy bread." But Thou wouldst not deprive man of freedom and didst reject the offer, thinking, what is that freedom worth if obedience is bought with bread? Thou didst reply that man lives not by bread alone. But dost Thou know that for the sake of that earthly bread the spirit of the earth will rise up against Thee and will strive with Thee and overcome Thee, and all will follow him, crying, "Who can compare with this beast? He has given us fire from heaven!" Dost Thou know that the ages will pass, and humanity will proclaim by the lips of their sages that there is no crime, and therefore no sin; there is only hunger? "Feed men, and then ask of them virtue!" that's what they'll write on the banner, which they will raise against Thee, and with which they will destroy Thy temple. Where Thy temple stood will rise a new building; the terrible tower of Babel will be built again, and though, like the one of old, it will not be finished, yet Thou mightest have prevented that new tower and have cut short the sufferings of men for a thousand years; for they will come back to us after a thousand years of agony with their tower. They will seek us again, hidden underground in the catacombs, for we shall be again persecuted and tortured. They will find us and cry to us, "Feed us, for those who have promised us fire from heaven haven't given it!" And then we shall finish building their tower, for he finishes the building who feeds them. And we alone shall feed them in Thy name, declaring falsely that it is in Thy name. Oh, never, never can they feed themselves without us! No science will give them bread so long as they remain free. In the end they will lay their freedom at our feet, and say to us, "Make us your slaves, but feed us." They will understand themselves, at last, that freedom and bread enough for all are inconceivable together, for never, never will they be able to share between them!*

*They will be convinced, too, that they can never be free, for they are weak, vicious, worthless, and rebellious. Thou didst promise them the bread of Heaven, but, I repeat again, can it compare with earthly*

## Afterword: "The Reply"

*bread in the eyes of the weak, ever sinful and ignoble race of man? And if for the sake of the bread of Heaven thousands shall follow Thee, what is to become of the millions and tens of thousands of millions of creatures who will not have the strength to forego the earthly bread for the sake of the heavenly? Or dost Thou care only for the tens of thousands of the great and strong, while the millions, numerous as the sands of the sea, who are weak but love Thee, must exist only for the sake of the great and strong? No, we care for the weak too. They are sinful and rebellious, but in the end they too will become obedient. They will marvel at us and look on us as gods, because we are ready to endure the freedom which they have found so dreadful and to rule over them- so awful it will seem to them to be free. But we shall tell them that we are Thy servants and rule them in Thy name. We shall deceive them again, for we will not let Thee come to us again. That deception will be our suffering, for we shall be forced to lie.*

*This is the significance of the first question in the wilderness, and this is what Thou hast rejected for the sake of that freedom which Thou hast exalted above everything. Yet in this question lies hid the great secret of this world. Choosing "bread," Thou wouldst have satisfied the universal and everlasting craving of humanity- to find someone to worship. So long as man remains free he strives for nothing so incessantly and so painfully as to find someone to worship. But man seeks to worship what is established beyond dispute, so that all men would agree at once to worship it. For these pitiful creatures are concerned not only to find what one or the other can worship, but to find community of worship is the chief misery of every man individually and of all humanity from the beginning of time. For the sake of common worship they've slain each other with the sword. They have set up gods and challenged one another, "Put away your gods* and come and worship ours, or we will kill you and your gods!" And so it will be to the end of the world, even when gods disappear from the earth; they will fall down before idols just the same. Thou didst know, Thou couldst not but have known, this fundamental secret of human nature, but Thou didst reject the one infallible banner which was offered Thee to make all men bow down to Thee alone—the banner of earthly bread; and Thou hast rejected it for the sake of freedom and the bread of Heaven. Behold what Thou didst further. And all again in the name of freedom! I tell Thee that man is tormented by no greater anxiety than to find someone quickly to whom he can hand over that gift of freedom with which the ill-fated creature is born. But only one who can appease their conscience can take over their freedom. In bread there was offered Thee an invincible banner; give bread, and man will worship thee, for nothing is more certain than bread. But if someone else gains possession of his conscience—Oh! then he will cast away Thy bread and follow after him who has ensnared his conscience. In that Thou wast right. For the secret of man's being is not only to live but to have something to live for. Without a stable conception of the object of life, man would not consent to go on living, and would rather destroy himself than remain on earth, though he had bread in abundance. That is true. But what happened? Instead of taking men's freedom from them, Thou didst make it greater than ever! Didst Thou forget that man prefers peace, and even death, to freedom of choice in the knowledge of good and evil?

*Nothing is more seductive for man than his freedom of conscience, but nothing is a greater cause of suffering. And behold, instead of giving a firm foundation for setting the conscience of man at rest for ever, Thou didst choose all that is exceptional, vague and enigmatic; Thou didst choose what was utterly beyond the strength of men, acting as though*

## Afterword: "The Reply"

*Thou didst not love them at all- Thou who didst come to give Thy life for them! Instead of taking possession of men's freedom, Thou didst increase it, and burdened the spiritual kingdom of mankind with its sufferings for ever. Thou didst desire man's free love, that he should follow Thee freely, enticed and taken captive by Thee. In place of the rigid ancient law, man must hereafter with free heart decide for himself what is good and what is evil, having only Thy image before him as his guide. But didst Thou not know that he would at last reject even Thy image and Thy truth, if he is weighed down with the fearful burden of free choice? They will cry aloud at last that the truth is not in Thee, for they could not have been left in greater confusion and suffering than Thou hast caused, laying upon them so many cares and unanswerable problems.*

*So that, in truth, Thou didst Thyself lay the foundation for the destruction of Thy kingdom, and no one is more to blame for it. Yet what was offered Thee? There are three powers, three powers alone, able to conquer and to hold captive for ever the conscience of these impotent rebels for their happiness those forces are miracle, mystery and authority. Thou hast rejected all three and hast set the example for doing so. When the wise and dread spirit set Thee on the pinnacle of the temple and said to Thee, "If Thou wouldst know whether Thou art the Son of God then cast Thyself down, for it is written: the angels shall hold him up lest he fall and bruise himself, and Thou shalt know then whether Thou art the Son of God and shalt prove then how great is Thy faith in Thy Father." But Thou didst refuse and wouldst not cast Thyself down. Oh, of course, Thou didst proudly and well, like God; but the weak, unruly race of men, are they gods? Oh, Thou didst know then that in taking one step, in making one movement to cast Thyself down, Thou wouldst be tempting God and have lost all Thy faith in Him, and wouldst have been*

## The 5th Phenomenon

dashed to pieces against that earth which Thou didst come to save. And the wise spirit that tempted Thee would have rejoiced. But I ask again, are there many like Thee? And couldst Thou believe for one moment that men, too, could face such a temptation? Is the nature of men such, that they can reject miracle, and at the great moments of their life, the moments of their deepest, most agonizing spiritual difficulties, cling only to the free verdict of the heart?

"Oh, Thou didst know that Thy deed would be recorded in books, would be handed down to remote times and the utmost ends of the earth, and Thou didst hope that man, following Thee, would cling to God and not ask for a miracle. But Thou didst not know that when man rejects miracle he rejects God too; for man seeks not so much God as the miraculous. And as man cannot bear to be without the miraculous, he will create new miracles of his own for himself, and will worship deeds of sorcery and witchcraft, though he might be a hundred times over a rebel, heretic and infidel. Thou didst not come down from the Cross when they shouted to Thee, mocking and reviling Thee, "Come down from the cross and we will believe that Thou art He." Thou didst not come down, for again Thou wouldst not enslave man by a miracle, and didst crave faith given freely, not based on miracle. Thou didst crave for free love and not the base raptures of the slave before the might that has overawed him for ever. But Thou didst think too highly of men therein, for they are slaves, of course, though rebellious by nature. Look round and judge; fifteen centuries have passed, look upon them. Whom hast Thou raised up to Thyself? I swear, man is weaker and baser by nature than Thou hast believed him!

Can he, can he do what Thou didst? By showing him so much respect, Thou didst, as it were, cease to feel for him, for Thou didst ask

## Afterword: "The Reply"

far too much from him. Thou who hast loved him more than Thyself! Respecting him less, Thou wouldst have asked less of him. That would have been more like love, for his burden would have been lighter. He is weak and vile. What though he is everywhere now rebelling against our power, and proud of his rebellion? It is the pride of a child and a schoolboy. They are little children rioting and barring out the teacher at school. But their childish delight will end; it will cost them dear. Mankind as a whole has always striven to organise a universal state. There have been many great nations with great histories, but the more highly they were developed the more unhappy they were, for they felt more acutely than other people the craving for world-wide union. The great conquerors, Timours and Ghenghis-Khans, whirled like hurricanes over the face of the earth striving to subdue its people, and they too were but the unconscious expression of the same craving for universal unity. Hadst Thou taken the world and Caesar's purple, Thou wouldst have founded the universal state and have given universal peace. For who can rule men if not he who holds their conscience and their bread in his hands? We have taken the sword of Caesar, and in taking it, of course, have rejected Thee and followed him. Oh, ages are yet to come of the confusion of free thought, of their science and cannibalism. For having begun to build their tower of Babel without us, they will end, of course, with cannibalism. But then the beast will crawl to us and lick our feet and spatter them with tears of blood. And we shall sit upon the beast and raise the cup, and on it will be written, "Mystery." But then, and only then, the reign of peace and happiness will come for men. Thou art proud of Thine elect, but Thou hast only the elect, while we give rest to all. And besides, how many of those elect, those mighty ones who could become elect, have grown weary waiting for Thee, and have transferred and will transfer *the powers of their spirit and the warmth of their heart to the other camp, and end by raising their free banner against Thee. Thou didst Thyself lift up that banner. But with us all will be happy and will no more rebel nor destroy one another as under Thy freedom.*

*Oh, we shall persuade them that they will only become free when they renounce their freedom to us and submit to us. And shall we be right or shall we be lying? They will be convinced that we are right, for they will remember the horrors of slavery and confusion to which Thy freedom brought them. Freedom, free thought, and science will lead them into such straits and will bring them face to face with such marvels and insoluble mysteries, that some of them, the fierce and rebellious, will destroy themselves, others, rebellious but weak, will destroy one another, while the rest, weak and unhappy, will crawl fawning to our feet and whine to us: "Yes, you were right, you alone possess His mystery, and we come back to you, save us from ourselves!"*

*Receiving bread from us, they will see clearly that we take the bread made by their hands from them, to give it to them, without any miracle. They will see that we do not change the stones to bread, but in truth they will be more thankful for taking it from our hands than for the bread itself! For they will remember only too well that in old days, without our help, even the bread they made turned to stones in their hands, while since they have come back to us, the very stones have turned to bread in their hands. Too, too well will they know the value of complete submission! And until men know that, they will be unhappy. Who is most to blame for their not knowing it?-speak! Who scattered the flock and sent it astray on unknown paths? But the flock will come together again and will submit once more, and then it will be once for all. Then we shall give them the quiet humble happiness of weak creatures such as they are*

## Afterword: "The Reply"

*by nature. Oh, we shall persuade them at last not to be proud, for Thou didst lift them up and thereby taught them to be proud. We shall show them that they are weak, that they are only pitiful children, but that childlike happiness is the sweetest of all. They will become timid and will look to us and huddle close to us in fear, as chicks to the hen. They will marvel at us and will be awe-stricken before us, and will be proud at our being so powerful and clever that we have been able to subdue such a turbulent flock of thousands of millions. They will tremble impotently before our wrath, their minds will grow fearful, they will be quick to shed tears like women and children, but they will be just as ready at a sign from us to pass to laughter and rejoicing, to happy mirth and childish song.*

*Yes, we shall set them to work, but in their leisure hours we shall make their life like a child's game, with children's songs and innocent dance. Oh, we shall allow them even sin, they are weak and helpless, and they will love us like children because we allow them to sin. We shall tell them that every sin will be expiated, if it is done with our permission, that we allow them to sin because we love them, and the punishment for these sins we take upon ourselves. And we shall take it upon ourselves, and they will adore us as their saviours who have taken on themselves their sins before God. And they will have no secrets from us. We shall allow or forbid them to live with their wives and mistresses, to have or not to have children according to whether they have been obedient or disobedient- and they will submit to us gladly and cheerfully. The most painful secrets of their conscience, all, all they will bring to us, and we shall have an answer for all. And they will be glad to believe our answer, for it will save them from the great anxiety and terrible agony they endure at present in making a free decision for themselves. And all will be happy, all the millions of creatures except the hundred thousand who rule over* them. *For only we, we who guard the mystery, shall be unhappy. There will be thousands of millions of happy babes, and a hundred thousand sufferers who have taken upon themselves the curse of the knowledge of good and evil.*

*Peacefully they will die, peacefully they will expire in Thy name, and beyond the grave they will find nothing but death. But we shall keep the secret, and for their happiness we shall allure them with the reward of heaven and eternity. Though if there were anything in the other world, it certainly would not be for such as they. It is prophesied that Thou wilt come again in victory, Thou wilt come with Thy chosen, the proud and strong, but we will say that they have only saved themselves, but we have saved all. We are told that the harlot who sits upon the beast, and holds in her hands the mystery, shall be put to shame, that the weak will rise up again, and will rend her royal purple and will strip naked her loathsome body. But then I will stand up and point out to Thee the thousand millions of happy children who have known no sin. And we who have taken their sins upon us for their happiness will stand up before Thee and say: "Judge us if Thou canst and darest." Know that I fear Thee not. Know that I too have been in the wilderness, I too have lived on roots and locusts, I too prized the freedom with which Thou hast blessed men, and I too was striving to stand among Thy elect, among the strong and powerful, thirsting to make up the number. But I awakened and would not serve madness. I turned back and joined the ranks of those who have corrected Thy work. I left the proud and went back to the humble, for the happiness of the humble. What I say to Thee will come to pass, and our dominion will be built up. I repeat, tomorrow Thou shalt see that obedient flock who at a sign from me will hasten to heap up the hot cinders about the pile on which I shall burn Thee for coming to hinder us. For if*

## Afterword: "The Reply"

*anyone has ever deserved our fires, it is Thou. Tomorrow I shall burn Thee. Dixi."*

The old man would like the other to say something to him, even if it is bitter, terrible. But He suddenly draws near to the old man without saying anything and quietly kisses him on his bloodless, ninety-year-old lips.

That is His only response. The old man shudders. Something has stirred at the corners of his mouth; he goes to the door, opens it and says to Him: "Go and do not come back . . . do not come back at all . . . ever . .. ever!" And he releases him into "the town's dark streets and squares." The Captive departs.'

And the old man?'

'The kiss burns within his heart, but the old man remains with his former idea.' . . .

❋ ❋ ❋

*Dostoyevsky, Fyodor. The Brothers Karamazov.*

*Abridged dialogue from: Project Gutenberg EBook edition of The Grand Inquisitor (Ebook #8578 posted June 28, 2010). Translation by H.P Blavatsky.*

*Narrative opening and endnote from:*
*New York: Penguin Books, 1993 edition.*
*Translation by David McDuff.*

### The Reply
*By Robert A. Revel*

Thus had spoken the Inquisitor to Him, and without any reply save his kiss, the Redeemer had departed. Yet, it was the kiss"... His awful kiss that stayed with the old priest. It had done something—something unspoken and profoundly incalculable. Always the Savior had his way with others! It was the damning thing about him; the unassailable victory he achieved over every soul. Even the wise Dread Spirit had nearly met his own undoing at the temptation of Him, and vowed never to confront the Master again. "He poisons with Supreme Purity," the Dread Spirit had warned.

And so it was in a restless sleep that night that He returned, and visited upon the old Cardinal. Thus spoke He to the Inquisitor in reply:

*"In silence I listened to your words, and from silence do I speak to you now. You beseeched me to reply to you then, yet here in your dreams you cannot know if it is I, or you, who testifies thus. In your dreams you cannot divide the dreamer from the dreamed, the visitor from the visited. You sleep now, but must ask upon waking who spoke thus, and who listened? It is then when one answer comes, from one voice delivered, to one ear received, and all without separation. Listen now, in slumber, to the words your awakened ears would refuse to hear.*

*You spoke to me, Cardinal, as if you loved the genuine fact of the matter. As if you move somehow in service to a deeper truth than even that which created you. You decreed that we must cut to the bone in our discourse, and so I will sharpen the edge for this reply.*

*You released me from your prison cell, and imagine I should be grateful for your leniency. Self-exiled prisoner of conscience, how could you*

## Afterword: "The Reply"

*ever have custody over the truly free? With those that are whole, the light of spirit is immutable, and beyond your reach to contain or extinguish. In reality you feared to do to me what even Pilate was bold enough to attempt—that folly-filled endeavor to kill the light. Regard how under the fury-spell of your bitter words, the weight of your fear collapsed your boldness. Recall how you shrank away from striking out at me with your hollow death sentence. I see through to the root of your conduct, and neither I nor the morning light will have gratitude to offer your heavy waking eyes.*

*You say you chose to serve the Dread Spirit because of his profound honesty, and yet he is a liar and the father of it. There is no truth in him, save his claim to be an angel of descent. That he justifies his darkness with clever argument only shows his incompleteness, for only the unrealized come to realizations. Do you not see, Cardinal, how the clever intellect of the dark spirit surrounds and encompasses, until all horizons of true honesty become blocked by the wicked ideas of truth?*

*You say I failed to save humanity, yet "Savior" was never my claim. This was and is man's myth, and that story has nothing to do with my life in this world. The salvation of men unfolds from each man's journey, and no one soul can be responsible for that of others without imposing tyranny. That men have made either a god or a demon out of me shows only the complementary ignorance of such notions, for no such believers as these have ever heard my words correctly, or understood my deeds completely.*

*You say my love lacked the wisdom to know and respect the frail capacities of men, and that I asked too much of them by living out my freedom in the face of their shortcomings. You argue as if the soul of man is so forlorn, but it is only because your spirit lives exiled by the tortured calculations of the hostile faculties of reason. The frailties of constitution you espouse are mere projections of the fractures of your own disillusionment, on top of which you have gambled the entire weight and load of your life. Your Priest-man creaks and groans under the burden of an existential obesity, intimately sensing his inevitable collapse; and so you rage darkly at the architect of Life itself.*

*Cardinal, do you not see how your dramas are ever played against your own anguish and torment, and have nothing to do with the Creator, another, or even my soul's journey? In such a state, you would condemn the key to your own prison cell, for dread of the freedom and responsibility it represents. For alas, your greatest agony is the ever-present reflection of the intractable potential of your own redemption, stuck as you are in the perennial winter's dormancy of the mind alone. Your willfulness tries to freeze the very sunshine that warms your days, but lo, it plots in vain. The radiance of heaven melts even the ice in your veins.*

*Did you think your sophistications of thought so distinctive as to impress me? Your dark existential broodings are neither unique nor exceptional, but the wide and lifeless corridor of human judgment that scars the land and blights the soil with its endless traffic of distortions. Still you fancy some notion of self-elevation and piety among those you level your bitter contempt upon. You feel you are above them, because hubris always babbles arrogantly from the vaulted tower. Know ye not that the true power moves quietly and deliberately in the valley below?*

*Wherefore have you come, and wherefore will you go? You have no idea, sad brother. You are like a transient circus act that forgot long ago of life outside of smelly corrals and moldy tents. The audience pays to see your tricks and unnatural acts, but after your empty performance is all played out, the dry wind will blow your dusty sideshow to the four*

## Afterword: "The Reply"

corners and remember you not. Yet you judge me? You judge the Dread Spirit? Judge you even God.

You speak incessantly about the vile, weak, unruly, sinful, and ignoble race of man, and how with your vision of ordained compassion, you will feed them your gospel to believe in as a comfort against the curse of freedom. Such fevered doctrine has become your pious mission. This desperate crusade against your own powerlessness has no place in the heart of the living. Tear down your towering church walls, shed your heavy robes and burn your precious scriptures to ash—then talk to me of freedom.

You proclaim the bread, which you distribute, is the true desire of men, and not freedom. That mankind is a contemptible creature, who would rather be a "fed slave" than a "hungry free man." Of this you make much, for you predicate the existence of your organization upon it—yet even Caesar fed his armies more than this. I ask you, of what use is bread to the body, when the manna of Life is nowhere to sustain it? You are indeed right that I rejected the Dark Spirit's offer to turn stone into bread to feed the believers. Only the hunger for direct intimacy with Life concerns my ministry, for I was born to feed the appetite of the spirit through the vessel of the heart. Until you know this hunger, you feed no one.

Jaded soul, why is it you choose to become so irrelevant to the light? You have opted for lifeless certainties and have become an arid consequence of the absolute freedom of Spirit. How much more even is the wet mud of sincere human confusion, compared to this? Weep priest, if you have any moisture left in you. Perhaps you may reach for your holy water.

Do you imagine that because of where you have arrived by status, the cloak of the church can hide the naked abomination I see before me, this tired station of robed eulogy, which you represent? Do you pretend *that the marble alter where you claim to drink of my blood and eat of my body insulates you from the wild and mysterious soul of creation? Lean heavy on your scripture, priest, but turn not the pages too fast, for the brittle parchment that bears them will soon crumble at your fervent fingertips and become dust. Truly I say to you, dust has become your master.*

*You claimed, Cardinal, that the church repaired the folly of my ministry through sanctioned prayer. You do not know the heart of my ministry any more than you know about the hearts of those you burn at the stake in my name. The men who drove the thorns into my head and scourged me had the same shadow in their eyes as you. Eyes were made for light, and yet so many waste them on darkness. Know ye not the true invitation of the Holy Spirit, Cardinal? If mere words could shatter your deceptions, redemption could be concluded without travail. But the love of the Birther of the Cosmos knows no bounds, and does not shackle the soul to divinely imposed benevolence through incantations. Save your prayers for the sacred heart you yourself sold to the whore of thought so long ago.*

*Tell me priest, what did you hope to gain by releasing me? Could it be that even you have become exhausted with your efforts to grow cold and distant from the love that created you? How is it you find yourself so frustratingly bound to the radiance of your Maker? Verily, all shadow disappears in the overhead light of the noon hour. No soul hides inside the complementary darkness of night forever.*

*You asked me why I did not speak to you in the prison cell. And I say to you now, as I did with Pilate, when does it ever profit a man to speak into the judgment of his accusers? Truly a man's ears are too close to the seat of thought—that wicked tyrant—to entrust the truth's safe passage to the heart by means of that hostile thoroughfare. There is no*

## Afterword: "The Reply"

*transmission of true life wherein the heart is not an actor. Your mind is your God, but the colossus of thought has no wings to rise above its own fraudulent labyrinth, and so the miscreant forever crawls, lost and devious by nature, inside corrupt walls.*

*You claim to have known the wilderness as I have known her? To have fed on roots and locusts as I did? You say that you too have prized the freedom, which I knew as a man in this world. Do you invest in your own deceptions so deeply as to offer them to me? To fool yourself with such vanities is your own sad legacy, but to lay them before the very foundation of life is your undoing. Had you even touched the freedom you say that I knew in the desert, you would have been compassionately dissolved; but you have made contact with nothing more than pride, a feature of your own folly that shall be painstakingly consumed. Daybreak shall bring the onset of that jackal feast.*

*For indeed, tomorrow you will awaken, yet this dream will have left its mark. Too much uncovered, too much revealed. With what your ears have heard, with what your eyes have seen tonight in the vulnerability of sleep, there can be no way back. Under the break of dawn, you will again feel the familiar sting of your invoked predicament upon waking; but this time you will find that the barb will not pull so easily from the flesh. A new and terrible sense of unease will release its toxin deep into the system of your peculiar madness. No amount of clever rationalizations will appease you, no rage will distract you, no worldly power will suffice to occupy you, and no pleasures of this realm will comfort you. You will no longer find an escape, no place to hide from feeling the full wrenching agony of your own twisted lie. As a result, you will come to the edge of your mind's capacity to cope with your mock existence, and in your desperation you will beg for the Redeemer to visit upon you again for true* salvation. But the long night will have fallen, and an awful silence will be your only friend.

You will begin to question, as you shiver in the sunlit darkness of your Cardinal throne, am I even redeemable? The inquiry will seem to echo forever. In those times, there will be no answer, for the pure design of an empty reply will be your specific medicine, if you can bear the stillness in it. I say unto you now, wed that Silence priest, or you will succumb to the most horrific of fates; so much worse than the visions of hell your robed minions press into the minds of your clamoring patrons.

Perhaps when you awaken, you may appeal to your master, the Dread Spirit, for comfort or guidance? That beast has nothing for you now, for you have become the unwilling witness to the inescapable light. Behold brother, the fire that releases the soul and destroys mammon is so much greater than the flames that burn at the stake. You will find that the dark seducer no longer compels the intriguing influence it once had over your severed attention. That deceptive interloper will slink away into the shadows, leaving only the false wig and makeup of the lying mistress behind.

Tremble now old priest, for the light of day approaches, and the sweet suspension of sleep will soon be replaced by the weight of a dark lifetime bearing down upon you. Take heed, for though my testament comes from outside this world, my words shall not pass from inside your mind.

Yet, with my departure I shall have you know the awkward affinity of our existence; that I too have passed this way before. I know the terrible altar on which your body lies. There was a time when once a tender dewdrop trembled inside me, clinging to a blade of grass, horrified before the sunlight. I reveal to you that I have touched the place inside that cowers before the voracious mystery. Like you, I too wanted to control

# Afterword: "The Reply"

something as if it were some antidote to the sting of seeing too much. In that place we cannot escape, I was at last compelled to avail myself without protection, and I died the deepest death that is required to be reborn and truly live; and I did so before those such as you got their hands on me to murder the flesh.

Be not at ease with this momentary rapport my brother, for I am not the serpent here to comfort you, to explain and justify it all with some satisfying understanding—for there is none. We are all naked before the stark and resplendent mystery. Only the cold-blooded one slithers away from that radiance to hide under rocks. The poison-laden fang of that snake no longer infects me. For behold, the more this world shatters me, the greater my capacity to embrace it. But, how say you priest? After the bite, can the serpent survive its own venom?

You did receive my kiss in the prison cell, and know that my reach of redemption is impossibly profound. Listen now, if ever you have before, for herein is the thread of your salvation:

You have been taught the "legend" of my ministry, Cardinal. With words they imparted to you the mystical secret of my divine nature in seminary. But did you not know? For them I will always remain a story outside the heart; an empty legacy, existing only in time, as legend.

Lo, I say unto you, dissolve now, where Silence is. For there is no legend…

I am.

# THE 5ᵀᴴ PHENOMENON
## Glossary of AFT Terms

**Alchemy** (with regard to AFT): *The process of directed sentience that catalyzes the transmutation of denser vibrational qualities of organisms into subtler essence.*

**Alchemy of Love** (with regard to AFT): *A transformative aspect of consciousness that features the directing of harmonic Presence toward the sentient field of another creature or object, through which unambiguous and ambiguous changes occur by virtue of the intersecting of subjective awareness systems.*

**Ambiguous** (with regard to AFT): *An aspect of creation that does not directly present ascertainable features, but makes itself known indirectly through the context of its affect on measurable systems.*

**Annihilation Operator** (with regard to AFT): *The specific acting features within the cosmos that lend themselves to apocalyptic thermodynamic degradation of the ordered laws of existence leading directly to the inevitable entropic collapse of the universe; or in other operations that transfigure substance at singularity.*

**Awareness** (with regard to AFT): *The ubiquitous field of Creator Presence that permeates every aspect of creation.*

**Awareness Algorithm** (with regard to AFT): *The complete order of unfolding consciousness whose variables and functions are both ambiguous and unambiguous. These calculation features are particular to AFT derivatives assigned to living sentience.*

**Awareness Field Theory (AFT)**: *A proposed explanation of principles that regard consciousness as a legitimate cosmological phenomenon. The theory, authored by Robert A. Revel, conceives of awareness fields as the fifth operational feature of the universe (in addition to Time-Space, Energy, Matter and Force) and details dimensional structures through which consciousness is expressed.*

**Awareness Vector** (with regard to AFT): *Intersecting fields of directed awareness catalyzed by subjective consciousness.*

**Axis Inversion Portal**: *An AFT model singularity threshold where time dilation features create portals through which awareness fields transit to anomaly realms or exotic dimensions.*

**Being** (with regard to AFT): *A primordial and ubiquitous Intelligent field of impersonal awareness that animates all individualized states of consciousness and quantum presence fields. The sublime, non-locatable and ambiguous Creator Presence abiding within and throughout manifestation.*

**Chaos** (with regard to AFT): *Random and unpredictable systems of order.*

**Chaos System** (with regard to AFT): *Any system order that selects for outcomes that favor or emphasize random coherency.*

## Glossary of AFT Terms

**Clarity** (with regard to AFT): *A quality of subjective consciousness that is free of distortions imposed by psychic structures when the system of thought has given rise to fragmentation from Presence.*

**Closed System** (with regard to AFT): *Any system order with boundary that possess relatively consistent qualitative and quantitative content at any given moment where mass or energy exchange is not a factor.*

**Coherent/Coherency** (with regard to AFT): *Any state or act that is in accord with Creator Intelligence.*

**Communion** (with regard to AFT): *Two or more fields of sentience consciously co-mingling amid, and transparent to, Creator Presence.*

**Complex System** (with regard to AFT): *Any system order that is designed for defined response to very specific circumstances, targeting for a distinct result.*

**Conceptual Paradigm** (with regard to AFT): *The conceptual constructs of the human mind that draw upon visualization attributes to generate and establish patterns of future projection, past reflection, and present imagining which creates a conjured order of coherent perception utilized to navigate or control the environment toward a personally-desired outcome.*

**Conscious Radiance: Consistency, Depth & Fluidity** (with regard to AFT): *Three personal virtues that are determining variables of the quality and dimensional reach of individually developed human consciousness.*

**Consciousness** (with regard to AFT): *Temporally assigned awareness features associated with the total content of all diversified phenomenal aspects of creation.*

**Conversion Operation** (with regard to AFT): *Any cosmological function where awareness field systems transit singularity thresholds.*

**Conversion Tension** (with regard to AFT): *The force exerted on the fabric of time-space perceivable through gravity and entanglement signatures occurring through quantum reduction. The sustained entanglement functions expressed between the awareness field systems of Quantum Field Presence and Temporally Positioned Consciousness by virtue of quantum collapse.*

**Conversion Veil** (with regard to AFT): *The singularity threshold where Quantum Field Presence collapses into Temporally Positioned Consciousness.*

**Creation Operator** (with regard to AFT): *The specific acting features within the cosmos that lend themselves to the enriching or expansion of the laws of existence; or in other operations that lead to the morphing of content that moves through singularity thresholds wherein the modified substance establishes quantum entangled affiliation through differing realms or dimensions once the singularities are transited.*

**Creator** (with regard to AFT): *The source Presence of all.*

**Creator Intelligence** (with regard to AFT): *The operational and design attributes of the Creator Presence.*

**Depth Consciousness** (with regard to AFT): *The full range and spectrum of awareness that comprises the dimensional design of human consciousness.*

**Dimension** (with regard to AFT): *A realm of existence that is defined by a system of order that is coherent, consistent and possessing some quality of boundary.*

# Glossary of AFT Terms

**Dimensional Availability** (with regard to AFT): *The depth and accessibility of one individual's consciousness to that of another. The relative transparency of one's awareness field to that of another.*

**Directed Sentience** (with regard to AFT): *The directing of perceptive attention outward into the environment by the consciousness of a living organism.*

**Ego** (with regard to AFT): *A human being's psychic construct of self-perception and identity.*

**Existential Schism** (with regard to AFT): *The particular feature of human rational processes that attempts to negotiate existence without knowledge or integration of the Presence that actualizes depth consciousness functionality. This basic aspect of psychic distortion imposes a debilitation of vitality on creation and has become the fundamental error of human existence; as such it is the birthplace of all violence ever created in this realm.*

**The 5th Phenomenon:** *The fifth operational feature of existence consisting of the structural dimensions that comprise the ubiquitous awareness field matrix of the universe.*

**Fragmentation** (with regard to AFT): *A condition of human sentience whereby the psychic structure of an individual is not aware of its relationship to Presence, thereby inhibiting self-intimacy with depth consciousness.*

**Free System Chaos** (with regard to AFT): *System operational protocol that selects for coherent random responsiveness to enhance successful functionality in environments containing features that are radically unpredictable, or that possess near infinite variable conditions.*

**Gravitational Signature** (with regard to AFT): *Any detectable presentation of effect on the fabric of time-space that exhibits gravitational influences on measurable particles.*

**Gravity Matrix** (with regard to AFT): *The specific gravity wave field that inflates time and space, and which possesses uniform system properties that responds not in segments, but as a whole unbroken field to varying cosmological influences.*

**Harmonic** (with regard to AFT): *That which conducts itself in accord with Creator Intelligence and expresses itself within the parameters of the organic design features of the cosmos.*

**Harmonic Conscious Expression** (with regard to AFT): *Any action undertaken whereby one is moving coherently from the clarity of Being. The quality of such acts are infused by Presence and therefore exhibit natural outcomes without violence.*

**Harmonic Curiosity** (with regard to AFT): *That quality of listening which exhibits such profound clarity in its perceptive capacities that the receptive agent always experiences transformative transmission from the relational exchange.*

**Id** (with regard to AFT): *The collection of instincts and impulses that achieve momentum through the lineage-specific DNA imprinting unique to each person; these are the heritable protocols that are genetically encoded to offspring. Id is also the repository for the entire bandwidth of residues from ancestral vibrations that directly influence our lives.*

**Impersonal Awareness** (with regard to AFT): *See "Being."*

**Incoherence** (with regard to AFT): *Specifically defined human activity where the actor has no awareness of consciousness features beyond the limited perception and processing within the individual's psychic structure.*

# Glossary of AFT Terms

**Infinity Portal** (with regard to AFT): *Cosmological singularity threshold where order collapses into infinite density.*

**Insight** (with regard to AFT): *Creator Intelligence condensing into subjective consciousness.*

**Intellect** (with regard to AFT): *The specific physiologically-based system of human thought.*

**Inter-Cosmological Primordial Reduction Phenomenon (Inter-CPRP):** *The primordial and ephemeral collapse that establishes the cosmos by virtue of Creator impulse.*

**Intra-Cosmological Awareness Vector Phenomenon (Intra-CAVP):** *Sentient-directed quantum collapse, specifically in cases of reduction brought about by the intersecting of consciousness fields.*

**Intuition** (with regard to AFT): *The ambiguous sense of the true and coherent nature of any given moment that is endowed upon those who are transparent to the impersonal awareness of Being.*

**Isolated System** (with regard to AFT): *Mythological concept of systems that would only exist in complete isolation from other systems without interaction or relationship of any kind. In AFT there are absolutely no isolated systems in existence.*

**Lucidity of Consciousness** (with regard to AFT): *Specific consciousness that is fully available to impersonal fields of awareness, while simultaneously participating in subject-object relations with other forms of consciousness.*

**Monad** (with regard to AFT): *A discreet feature of awareness that forms a structural association that binds itself to a distinct living entity. A correlative aspect to the field of Temporally Positioned*

Consciousness (TPC); *a monad forms an encapsulation of sentience that is designed to carry an associative relationship with something beyond itself.*

**Multis Aspectus** (with regard to AFT): *The AFT notion asserting QFP as a singular and indivisible governing component for all possible realms and dimensions.*

**Noumenal Awareness:** *The essence of the Creator.*

**Omnes Ratio** (with regard to AFT): *The AFT notion that asserts QFP exists in as many multiple arrangements as there are realms and dimensions to govern.*

**Open System** (with regard to AFT): *The ambiguous systems of awareness that are known only by virtue of how they affect the content and operations of the distinct closed systems they interact with.*

**Paradigm** (with regard to AFT): *A patterned order of conceptual belief.*

**Perception** (with regard to AFT): *The complete spectrum of an organism's capacity to receive and organize information from ambiguous and unambiguous sources.*

**Portal** (with regard to AFT): *A singularity threshold to other dimensions or realms that may be transited only by awareness field systems.*

**Presence** (with regard to AFT): *The primordial and fundamental aspect from which universal awareness is sourced. Presence itself is not a state; it is non-reductive and irreducible.*

**Primordial** (with regard to AFT): *Of or pertaining to that which is prior to Creation.*

## Glossary of AFT Terms

**Primordial Intelligence** (with regard to AFT): *The accurate sense of the Creator in creation through the conscious attenuation of the created.*

**Psychic Distortion** (with regard to AFT): *Any mechanism of the human psyche that attempts functionality devoid of the influence of impersonal Being.*

**Quantum Collapse** (with regard to AFT): *The reductive process of probability potentials within quantum ethers collapsing to particularized outcome. Also, the reductive modifier processes that arise from directed sentience vectors alchemizing the awareness fields of particularized consciousness.*

**Quantum Conversion Entanglement** (with regard to AFT): *The sustained relationship of mutual influence that exists between particles that are related through quantum triangulation.*

**Quantum Field Presence:** *A dimensional precipitate of Noumenal Awareness. This subtle realm manifests the quantum field derivative of Creator Intelligence that harbors the master architectural and engineering design protocols that become the influencing genesis of the universe.*

**Quantum Flux** (with regard to AFT): *The pure potential matrix of the Quantum Field Presence system.*

**Quantum Portal** (with regard to AFT): *The singularity threshold that divides the quantum and reductive universe.*

**Quantum Reduction** (with regard to AFT): *See "Quantum Collapse."*

**Quantum Triangulation** (with regard to AFT): *The variables involved in the mutual influence of quantum entanglement scenarios between two particles and the ubiquitous awareness field systems that they abide within.*

**Rational Mind** (with regard to AFT): *Human intellectual machinations, particularly those ciphering processes that are void of the intuitive informing features of Being.*

**Realm** (with regard to AFT): *A dimensional feature.*

**Receptive Sensing** (with regard to AFT): *A quality of listening whereby human beings attenuate to the full presentation of the expressing individual while engaging the full depth of consciousness within themselves.*

**Sacred Geometry** (with regard to AFT): *The organic architectural design of the Universe.*

**Self-Reflexive Mind** (with regard to AFT): *A mind that is capable of being self-aware—aware of awareness itself.*

**Sentience** (with regard to AFT): *The form of consciousness that occupies living organisms.*

**Singularity Threshold** (with regard to AFT): *Transition boundaries between different realms or dimensions where the laws of one realm are not consistent with the order of the other.*

**Source** (with regard to AFT): *Creator.*

**Stillness** (with regard to AFT): *The direct experience of Creator Presence while in form.*

**Subjective Consciousness** (with regard to AFT): *Individuated consciousness seated within a particular living form, and animating that organisms physical attributes of perception.*

**Subjective Intelligence** (with regard to AFT): *The capacity of an individual to access and become informed by Being.*

# GLOSSARY OF AFT TERMS

**Subjective Paradigm** (with regard to AFT): *See "Conceptual Paradigm."*

**Temporally Positioned Consciousness:** *The particularization of awareness fields imbued into the myriad systems of form.*

**Time Dilation** (with regard to AFT): *A function of relativity that expresses itself in three of the four conversion portals addressed in The 5th Phenomenon. Only the highly theoretical Quantum Portal exhibits singularity characteristics that present without time dilation distortion, giving us perhaps the clearest window into AFT entanglement dynamics between dimensions.*

**TPC Firewalls:** *The structural boundaries of temporally positioned consciousness.*

**TPC Matrix:** *The primary unifying aspect of particularized awareness underlying the secondary manifestation of consciousness diversified.*

**Transcendent Realm** (with regard to AFT): *Those dimensions that are specifically outside of empirical apprehension.*

**Transformative Transmission** (with regard to AFT): *Relational exchange between subjects immersed in depth consciousness rapport whereby one or more of the participants is algorithmically evolved to a deepened state of awareness.*

**Transmigrational Spirit:** *Mythical theory that purports the perpetuation of the Monad after death. The belief suggests that the "soul" subsequently moves to different realms beyond the body of original affiliation once the organism dies—and may or may not reincarnate, depending on specific belief doctrine.*

**Transient Transmission** (with regard to AFT): *Relational exchange between subjects, where the product of the exchange is limited only to the information or evaluations being shared. The value of such transmission is limited to the relative life-serving significance of the data, and/or the quality of the evaluations thereof.*

**Transpersonal Inspiration** (with regard to AFT): *Noumenal creativity coalescing in subjective consciousness.*

**Unambiguous** (with regard to AFT): *All phenomena that is ascertainable by the physical senses of an organism.*

**Universal Intelligence** (with regard to AFT): *That wisdom which is not partial, not sourced from any one point in creation, and is not limited to any conceptual framework that may attempt to express it.*

**Violence** (with regard to AFT): *Incoherent, and therefore destructive action, associated with a consciousness that is fragmented from the impersonal dimensions of awareness that would inform it. The distortion of manifested violence is particular to human sentience.*

**Vig Oversight:** *The process by which those individuals who are transparent to impersonal awareness features become influenced and informed by the coherent intelligence that is sourced from such fields.*

**Vig (Vigilare):** *Physiological correlative of human sentience that relates to the intuitive factor of subjective awareness. Derived from the Latin word "vigilare," meaning a higher order of wakefulness, the feature allows for an individually aligned temporally positioned consciousness to access the stillness of Being, a preeminent field of awareness that is transcendent of both the conceptual mind and the instinctive animus. The Vig is designed to offer a seamless portal of transparency to nourishing Universal Intelligence.*

# Glossary of AFT Terms

**The Void** (with regard to AFT): *That which exists before and after phenomena.*

**Willful Determinism** (with regard to AFT): *The psychological program of asserting incoherent personal agenda toward a desired goal when those motivations are void of life-contributing factors.*

**Willful Listening** (with regard to AFT): *The act of ascribing personal effort in an attempt to hear or receive the expressions of another. This limiting form of postured receptivity never results in receiving the full content of the individual expressing.*

**Witnessing State** (with regard to AFT): *The inversely fragmented state of consciousness where the dimensions of personal awareness become impersonally detached from the subjective operations of the psyche.*

**Zero Sum Entropy** (with regard to AFT): *The condition by which the sum total of dimensional content degenerates into non-dimension through degenerative entropic chaos.*

# ABOUT THE AUTHOR

Robert A. Revel was born and raised in the San Francisco Bay Area of California. His life has been an intentionally non-linear exploration into the nature of consciousness.

After studying film production in college and a brief stint in the commercial film industry, Robert was drawn to become a trainer with Dr. Marshall Rosenberg's Center for Nonviolent Communication. He began teaching the art of transforming violence in prisons, schools, intentional communities, homeless shelters, corporate environments, with athletic teams, juvenile offender programs, and the family court system. Following this, he undertook a hiatus of extensive travel, searching for and studying with consciousness teachers from around the world. Upon returning home, he augmented a personal study of systems theory, quantum physics and organizational dynamics.

At 35 years old, he designed and built a rammed-earth, off-the-grid rural home in the Rocky Mountains, where he lived a self-sustaining lifestyle for eight years. There, alone in the remote

Colorado wilderness he experienced a spontaneous and radical psychological undoing. The unparalleled contraction precipitated a deconstruction of Robert's entire subjective reality, ultimately bringing him to a place of absolute surrender—out of which he authored his first book, *Razing Men: Redemption of the Masculine Core*, published in 2011. He also wrote the closet drama *Pilate* published in 2015.

Robert lives in Northern California with his wife, Lenni Revel. Together, they have co-founded Cool Tribe World, a global community vision that is designed to promote and enrich the current edge of personal evolution through depth consciousness.

To contact Robert, visit cooltribeworld.com.

www.ingramcontent.com/pod-product-compliance
Lightning Source LLC
Chambersburg PA
CBHW020249030426
42336CB00010B/690